Kinky's
CELEBRITY
PET FILES

KINKY FRIEDMAN

SIMON & SCHUSTER   New York • London • Toronto • Sydney

Simon & Schuster
1230 Avenue of the Americas
New York, NY 10020

First Simon & Schuster hardcover edition October 2009

SIMON & SCHUSTER and colophon are registered trademarks
of Simon & Schuster, Inc.

Photo credits and permissions can be found on page 207.

Text reprint permissions: "Mr. Bojangles." Words and music by Jerry
Jeff Walker. ©1968 (renewed) Cotillion Music, Inc. and MIJAC Music.
All rights administered by Warner-Tamerlane Publishing Corp.;
"What's in a Name?" from *Molly Ivins Can't Say That Can She?* by
Molly Ivins, copyright © 1991 by Molly Ivins. Used by permission of
Random House, Inc.; "Pickin' Time." Words and music by Johnny Cash.
Copyright notice: © 1958 (renewed) Chappell & Co., Inc. All rights
reserved. Used by permission of Alfred Music Publishing Co., Inc.

For information about special discounts for bulk purchases, please
contact Simon & Schuster Special Sales at 1-866-506-1949 or
business@simonandschuster.com

The Simon & Schuster Speakers Bureau can bring authors to your
live event. For more information or to book an event contact the
Simon & Schuster Speakers Bureau at 1-866-248-3049 or visit our
website at www.simonspeakers.com.

Designed by Dana Sloan

Manufactured in the United States of America

10 9 8 7 6 5 4 3 2 1

Library of Congress Cataloging-in-Publication Data
Friedman, Kinky.
   Kinky's celebrity pet files / Kinky Friedman.
      p. cm.
1. Pets of celebrities. 2. Pets. 3. Celebrities. I. Title.
   SF411.5 F75— 2009
   636.088'7—dc22   2009012330

ISBN 978-1-4767-5477-2

ACKNOWLEDGMENTS

THE AUTHOR WOULD like to thank the many celebrities who agreed to participate in this book, and place an ancient Hebrew curse upon the few who didn't. It should also be noted, unfortunately, that a number of willing celebrities did not make it into the Celebrity Pet Files simply because the harried, irritated author had to virtually fend off suicide while attempting to bring together celebrities, pets, photographers, editors, and lawyers all in time for publishing deadlines.

Ah yes, it was a herculean, as well as somewhat tedious task, but I did learn three things: 1) Animals are more pleasant to deal with than people, 2) Animals, celebrities, photographers, and editors are more pleasant to deal with than lawyers, and 3) Ernest Hemingway was right: Fame is death's little sister.

On that cheerful note, let me thank the dedicated, intrepid crew who helped penetrate the private lives of the rich, the famous, and the kind. The following are some of the folks who have made this charming, challenging voyage in a paper boat possible: Nina Schwartz, editor, and David Rosenthal (Simon & Schuster); David Vigliano, agent; Debora Hanson, Max Swafford, Kent Perkins, Sally Parks, Van Dyke Parks, Melinda Wilson, Cousin Nancy, Susan Walker, Cynthia Merman, Jonathan Sandys, Valerie Heller, Carolyn Farb, Larry "Ratso" Sloman, Chicken Dick, Mitch Blank, Michelle Press, Amelie Frank, Stephanie Chernikowski, Marty Stuart, Laurie Hutton, Kay Northcott, Judy Dierker, Betsy Moon, Reverend Goat Carson, Bud Shrake, Ellen Richards, Cat Rebennak, Dr. Kathleen Hudson, St. Francis, Chuck E. Weiss, the Buddha, and, of course, the Friedmans.

THIS BOOK IS DEDICATED TO THE STRAYS AND TO THE ONES WHO PROTECT THEM.

What is man without the beasts? If all the beasts were gone, men would die from great loneliness of spirit, for whatever happens to the beast also happens to the man.
—*Chief Seattle, 1855*

A farting horse never tires.
—*Willie Nelson, 2009*

CONTENTS

CONTENTS

KINKY'S
CELEBRITY
PET FILES

INTRODUCTION

Dear Reader,

The Lord has commanded me to write a celebrity pet book. Like a good little church worker, I always try to follow all of God's commandments that I like. I remember His voice quite clearly as it came to me several years ago while I was polishing the Luger I'd bought from a former U-boat commander. The conversation, as near as I recall, went something like this:

GOD: Kinkstah!

KF: Start talkin'.

GOD: I am the Lord Thy God.

KF: Shit. I thought you were my agent.

GOD: In a sense, I suppose, I am thy agent. Let's see. I believe you're up to twenty-seven books. That's twenty-two more than Moses.

KF: Twenty-eight! I've written twenty-eight!

GOD: Hold the weddin', son. You don't really expect me to

1

count that last one where you throw the lesbian off the bridge and then kill yourself? Lesbians are my children too, you know.

KF: Who *is* this?

GOD: In this time of great trouble in the land, like everything and everyone else, book sales are suffering. The only books that are selling are books about celebrities and books about pets, and, of course, my book's still doing pretty well.

KF: Sure your book's doing well—it was ghostwritten by Janet Evanovich.

GOD: (*chuckles good-naturedly*) Kinkstah! I command you to write a celebrity pet book! And I command you to do it without including Paris Hilton and her pretentious pedigreed poodle!

KF: What! That's impossible! It can't be done!

GOD: Thus saith the Lord!

And so, dear reader, that was exactly how it went, and here you are reading the author's introduction and wondering where the hell is Paris Hilton and her pretentious pedigreed poodle, and now you know why they aren't in the book. As for the people and pets who did make the cut, however, I can say only this: "Some are dead and some are living, and in my life I've loved them all."

Kinky Friedman
Texas Hill Country
Jan. 10, 2009

JERRY JEFF WALKER and COCO

WHILE I'VE NEVER been a really big fan of pedigreed dogs in general, I've always been a really big fan of Jerry Jeff Walker's. And, I have to admit, some Maltese are very smart and very cool. Furthermore, whether or not a dog happens to be pedigreed is never his or her fault. But I'll let Jerry Jeff explain the situation in his own words.

"Coco comes from a breeder in Ireland," he told me, "who only sells to European clients. Friends of ours got her and delivered her to us while my wife Susan and I were staying at the Ritz in Paris. Coco Chanel had lived there for years with her dogs. The Ritz could not turn us down for having a puppy when we reminded them of that. So, in honor of Coco Chanel, we named her Coco.

"Coco is actually my wife's dog—or was at one time. I have managed to steal her unwavering affection by feeding her people food and totally acknowledging that she is the mistress of the house. Ever since Susan got her in Paris eight years ago, she's traveled with us everywhere. She is a very worldly dog. Like me, however, she now prefers to stay close to home and make sure everything is in its place."

Johnny Donnels, whom Jerry Jeff refers to as "the infamous New Orleans photographer," took this early photo when the Walkers lived in New Orleans and Coco was just a puppy. Donnels not only took the photo but was also, apparently, quite taken with Coco. Of his subject he adds, "She has a French tattoo in her right ear, so she has dual citizenship. And she flies first class."

"We were talking the other day," says Jerry Jeff, "about what breeds of dogs do. The Maltese is bred to sit in your lap and snuggle. Coco is purebred and has these traits down pat. Because she's traveled so much, she knows about suitcases. When I pack for the road, she hops in before I'm finished. I have to sneak out. But there have been some driveways of life that I've had to back out of with my lights off."

There's another dog in Jerry Jeff's life, one he heard about only in a cell in New Orleans when he was down and out. This dog had no pedigree. He later would immortalize the dog and his human companion in one of the most recorded songs of all time, "Mr. Bojangles," a simple, perfect verse of which follows.

He danced for those in minstrel shows and county fairs
throughout the South

"I hate it when he does this!"

He spoke with tears of fifteen years how his dog and him
*   traveled about*
His dog up and died, he up and died
After twenty years he still grieves
*   Mr. Bojangles*
*   Mr. Bojangles*
*   Mr. Bojangles*
*   Dance.*

Jerry Jeff wrote this song in Austin in the mid-sixties, when he was practically a homeless person with a guitar. Looking back, it is hard to believe that a Nashville record executive once passed on the song, remarking at the time, "Nobody wants to hear a song about an old drunk nigger and a dead dog."

"Mr. Bojangles was actually white," Jerry Jeff told me. "If he'd been black, I never would've met him. The prison was segregated."

I asked Jerry Jeff to tell me about writing "Mr. Bojangles." This is what he said: "I'd been reading a lot of Dylan Thomas, and I was really into the concept of internal rhyme. I just had my guitar, a yellow pad, and the memories of guys I'd met in drunk tanks and on the street—one gentle old man in particular. The rest of the country was listening to the Beatles, and I was writing a six-eight waltz about an old man and hope. It was a love song.

"During the time I was writing 'Mr. Bojangles', I used to go down to the Austin city pound about every two weeks and adopt a dog. I didn't really live anywhere myself, so the dog often stayed with me awhile and then it would run away. Maybe find somebody else. At least I felt I was giving him a second chance."

"I know who you are, and I saw what you did."

MURRAY LANGSTON, THE UNKNOWN COMIC

MURRAY LANGSTON IS an old friend of mine. He's also one of the most talented, most independent, toughest, and funniest people I know. Imagine surviving, often thriving, in Hollywood for four decades appearing in more than eight hundred TV shows and movies without ever having an agent or a manager, and much of the time with a paper bag over your head.

This is precisely what Murray Langston, aka the Unknown Comic, has been able to accomplish; he has navigated the dangerous, deceptive currents of life and show business, in high tides and in low, always maintaining a brilliant sense of humor. There are two kinds of sailors, I've often thought: the sailor who fights the sea, and the sailor who loves the sea. Murray loves the sea. I'll let him tell you in his own words, as he told it to me.

"I got on *Laugh-In*, a big, popular TV show, by just calling them up. It was 1970 and I was very naïve. 'How can I get on that show?' I asked, and they said, 'Do something unusual.' They had me on four times. I did an impression of a fork, a tube of toothpaste, a grandfather clock, and something else I've forgotten. After that it was the typical Hollywood story: I didn't work for three years.

"Then I started doing sketches at a club owned by Redd Foxx, hanging out with guys like Cheech and Chong before they made it. I formed a comedy team with a guy named Freeman King and some producers saw us at Redd's club, and for the next four and a half years I was on the *Sonny & Cher Show*.

"Then I had some money so I bought a nightclub in North Hollywood where I specialized in ribs and later in bankruptcy. My club was the first place David Letterman worked in L.A. Debra Winger was one of my waitresses.

"After I lost the club I was broke, and *The Gong Show* was a big hit, with many actors who needed money going on. I didn't want anybody to know it was me because I'd just been on *The Sonny & Cher Show*. I figured I'd put a paper bag on my head and call myself the Unknown Comic. I'd do a couple jokes and get my couple hundred dollars. That's all I meant to do. But what I did is, I came out and insulted the creator and host of the show, Chuck Barris. I did a few jokes and then said, 'Hey, Chuck, do you and your wife ever make love in the shower?' And he said, 'No.' I said, 'Well, you should. She loves it.' The audience loved it, too. So he wanted me to come back and insult him again. I did maybe forty or fifty television shows like that, as the Unknown Comic.

"Things got so hot I contacted Vegas and got a booking at the Sahara. I had a band with bags over their heads and dancers with bags over their heads. I was getting paid five grand a week, and the show was costing me six grand a week. But I had to do something because I had no real act. It took me a year to develop an act and I could slowly let everybody go, and then I started making money. But in the beginning that's what people wanted to see, the whole show was this bag character.

"One night Freeman King and I went backstage to see my friend, the singer Bobbie Gentry. She said, 'I want you to meet a friend of mine.' We go, 'Holy jeez.' It was Elvis. Anyway, we start talking to him and he says, 'Come on, we'll go to my place, have a party.' This was Vegas, so we go to his suite in the Hilton. He's doing karate moves on me and I'm always making him laugh and every time I made him laugh my brain would go, 'You just made Elvis Presley laugh.' It was the freakiest thing. We were there for hours. We sat on the floor and he's sitting right next to me singing, 'Are You Lonesome Tonight?' You couldn't believe you're sitting next to Elvis while he's singing. At about five in the morning he started doing Bible songs and that's when we got going.

"I've also been threatened by Frank Sinatra. I never did Sinatra jokes in my act, but I did one joke on television where I said, 'Sinatra's gonna open a halfway house for girls who don't go all the way.' I totally forgot about it and later I'm home shaving and he calls me on the phone. Of course, you don't think Sinatra's calling you. So I pick up the phone and he goes, 'Is this Murray Langston?' I go, 'Yeah.' He says, 'This is Sinatra, you cocksucker,' and he starts cursing me. 'You ever mention my name, I'm going to break your fucking legs.' That kind of thing. I don't believe it's Sinatra, I think it's a friend of mine.

"I'm going, 'Fuck you, dickhead.' He's going back and forth with me and I'm laughing at him, and the more I laugh at him, the more he's getting pissed off. He's screaming at me, saying, 'This is Frank Sinatra.' So I say, 'Yeah, if you're Sinatra, sing "My Way," asshole.'

"That's what did it. He just yelled at me and hung up. So I go back to shaving and a few minutes later the phone rings again and I pick it up. It's another voice I recognize, saying, 'Is this Murray Langston?' I say, 'Yeah.' He says, 'This is Uncle Miltie. Milton Berle. Do you recognize my voice?' I tell him I recognize his voice. He says, 'Look, Frank just called me. Apparently you didn't think you were talking to him.' I had to stop shaving because I probably would've cut my throat.

"I love Kinky Friedman, but you take away his looks, you

take away his money, and you take away his talent, and what do you have?

"Before becoming the Unknown Comic, I used to be a stuntman in porno films, but I only had a small part. My most notable film was *King Kong Plays Ping Pong with His Ding Dong in Hong Kong.*"

P.S. Murray informs me that his cat is named Pussy.

"Shh . . . If we don't look at her, maybe she'll go away."

WINSTON CHURCHILL *and* RUFUS

THERE IS VERY little worth saying in this world that hasn't already been said by either Mark Twain, Oscar Wilde, or Winston Churchill. Though all three indubitably had their favorite pets, and I use that word loosely, Churchill was by far the most avid animal lover. It is no wonder that this wise and witty warrior was able to weather the wrath of the Wehrmacht so well. He knew that in life success was never final and failure rarely fatal and what was important was what you did after that. Much of Churchill's personal strength and iron will, widely acknowledged to have played a major part in pulling England through the dark days of World War II, can be attributed, I believe, in no small part to the comfort and spiritual stamina of a soul that shares its life and its love with animals.

As for the wit of the man, the incidents are legend and legion. There was the time Churchill was in the upstairs loo, in the words of my friend the Reverend Goat Carson, "letting the possum out." An annoying politician came to the front door and, with great urgency, prevailed upon the servant to give the message to the prime minister that he must see him immediately. When the servant dutifully went upstairs and relayed the message, the great man is said to have responded, "I can only take one shit at a time."

Then there was the time when George Bernard Shaw was opening a new play in London. The playwright and Churchill were not fond of each other, but the play's producers prevailed upon Shaw to send Churchill an invitation to opening night. Shaw sent the invitation, scrawling a personal note at the bottom, "Bring a friend, if you have one."

Churchill wrote back expressing his regrets that he couldn't make opening night. At the bottom he wrote, "Will attend a later performance, if there is one."

Winston Churchill smoked more cigars than there are crossties on the railroad or stars in the sky, yet he lived to be ninety. The only commoner given a state funeral, he never wanted honors, yet they were heaped upon him. For the purposes of this book, however, I wanted to know more about this iconic man and his deep, abiding devotion to the animal kingdom. So much has been written about Churchill that, after years of exhaustive research, it became impossible for me to decipher the myth from the reality. To hell with Hitler and Stalin! I wanted to know about Rufus.

Finally, with the help of my friend Carolyn Farb, I was able to get to the source. She arranged for me to conduct an interview with the man who knows things about England's wartime leader that stuffy scholars only dream of. His name is Jonathan Sandys and he is Winston Churchill's great-grandson. We met at Kenny & Ziggy's deli in Houston. Unfortunately, no notebooks or tape recordings are allowed because somebody might eat them. I had the good sense not to ask the question that was foremost on my mind: Why do newborn babies all seem to bear an uncanny resemblance to his great-grandfather? Instead, we focused on Churchill's love for animals.

"Great-Grandpapa," said Jonathan, "was getting ready to carve the turkey for Christmas lunch. That's dinner to you. Before he starts he asks where the turkey is from, and his wife, Clementine, says 'It's one of ours, dear.' Great-Grandpapa puts down the fork and carving knife. 'One cannot eat something that one has been on speaking terms with,' he says."

Indeed, according to Jonathan, Chartwell was never a working farm because "Great-Grandpapa refused to allow an animal to be slaughtered once he had said 'Good morning' to it."

Jonathan quotes Churchill as stating, "The nose of the

bulldog has been slanted backward so that he can breathe without letting go."

He also quotes his great-grandfather regarding his fondness for pigs: "Dogs look up to you. Cats look down on you. Give me a pig. He just looks you in the eye and treats you like an equal."

Then, of course, there was Rufus, the black poodle who was especially close to Churchill's heart. Rufus ate with the rest of the family. He had his own special tablecloth on the Persian carpet. On Churchill's orders, no one started eating until Rufus had his food laid out.

Churchill had birds, fish, chickens, cows, horses (his last polo pony, Energy, retired in 1926), rare black swans (a gift from Southern Australia only to himself and the queen), geese, turkeys, sheep, pigs, and, of course, a succession of beloved dogs and cats. His nickname for himself was Mr. Pug the pig. Clementine was Pussycat.

Finally, Jonathan told me about an incident that occurred during a trip his great-grandfather made to America. It is only peripherally related to animals, but I feel it is worthy of inclusion.

"He was invited to a fancy luncheon in Virginia. When asked what part of the chicken he wanted, he said, 'I'll have a bit of breast.' The hostess replied, 'We don't say breast; we say white meat or dark meat.'

"The next day, he sent her a corsage with the following message: 'I'd be obliged if you would attach this to your white meat.'"

Jonathan Sandys is the founder of Churchill's Britain, a foundation that works to promote his great-grandfather's ideals, values, and inspirational life story. For more information, go to churchillsbritainfoundation.org.

"What do you think about calling our fans 'manatee-heads'?"

JIMMY BUFFETT *and* THE MANATEE

ONE MORNING IN Los Angeles in 1976, Jimmy Buffett and I were having breakfast together. As I remember, we both had eggs Benedict, which I referred to as eggs bend-my-dick. We both had recording contracts with a company called ABC-Dunhill, which I referred to as ABC-Dunghill. We were both commiserating about how hard it was to break into the music business. We didn't know it then, but things were about to change.

Within a few months Bob Dylan invited me to join him on the road with his Rolling Thunder Revue. Shortly thereafter, Jimmy released an album titled *Changes in Latitudes, Changes in Attitudes*. It contained a wistful, catchy little song called "Margaritaville," which soon took off like a rocket and made some major changes in Jimmy's bank account. Many years later, in reviewing Jimmy's novel *A Salty Piece of Land* for the *New York Times*, I began with the following sentence: "There's a fine line between fiction and nonfiction, and I believe Jimmy Buffett and I snorted it in 1976."

Jimmy is one of the few artists I know who were able to take a monstro-hit and not become a one-hit wonder; instead, more than thirty years later, he's taken a monstro-hit and built it into a monstro-career. Few if any performers today can sell out a large venue faster than Jimmy Buffett and the Coral Reefers. This enduring popularity and loyalty, far and above merely being a financial pleasure, certainly must be regarded as its own personal reward for any artist.

Thus I was pleasantly surprised, during the heat of my 2006 independent campaign for governor of Texas, to get a call on my cell phone from Jimmy offering to help our efforts. This is in keeping with his long-standing passion for political reform and protecting the environment. Like a true musician—not a politician—Jimmy asked for nothing in return. Well, that's almost correct.

"If you're elected governor," he said, "I only want one thing."

"What's that?" I asked.

"Port Aransas," he said.

My friend Rick Reichenbach, the lighthouse keeper for the little town of Port Aransas, near Corpus Christi, thought it was a hell of a good idea. "Just cede Port Aransas to Jimmy Buffett for four years," he said, "and it'd result in the biggest economic and tourist boom the town has ever seen."

I never got a chance to make good on that deal, but, for his part, Jimmy did. He raised more than $250,000 for our campaign at a show at the Paramount theater in Austin. The show sold out in about five minutes.

Not only is Jimmy Buffett a highly successful entrepeneur, musician, author, and seaplane pilot, there's something else about him that will always give him a special place in my heart. More than any other single human being, he has given the most time, money, and effort toward saving the manatee.

The Save the Manatee Club, founded by Jimmy and Senator Bob Graham in 1981, is the best way for the public to participate in helping to conserve the population and the habitat of these harmless, lovable, and highly endangered marine animals. The population of manatees in Florida is thought to be between one thousand and three thousand, but the number of manatee deaths caused by humans has been increasing over the years.

If you want to help Jimmy save the manatees, go to savethemanatee.org. You'll be glad you did.

"I've got the best seat in the house."

JOSEPH HELLER and PHILIPPE

THE FIRST TIME I saw Joseph Heller I fell in love with him. It was the dead of winter in 1981, and though he was almost completely paralyzed in a hospital bed, I could tell by the feverish look in his eyes that he had definitely taken a turn for the nurse. I didn't know it then, but I would soon become good friends with the literary genius who gave the world *Catch-22*, and also with the nurse, who would soon become Mrs. Valerie Heller.

I met Joe in the first place through the good offices of my good friend Speed Vogel, who'd once been a roommate of Mel Brooks. Neil Simon, upon observing the ridiculous, ill-suited nature of their relationship, is said to have based *The Odd Couple* on the two of them.

Speed called me one day and said Heller wanted to use my name and character in a new book he was working on. The book was titled *Good as Gold*.

"Great," I remember telling Speed. "How much will he pay?"

"That," said Speed, "I can tell you right now. Not a fucking nickel."

Catch-22 had become an international phenomenon, regarded by many readers, myself included, as a secular bible. Some critics even suggested that Heller would never write another book as good as *Catch-22*. To this, Joe always modestly responded, "No one else will either."

"It was 1953," Heller told me, "and I was hunched over my desk in an advertising agency. It took eight years to write and I never called it *Catch-22*; I called it *Catch-18*. I even published the first chapter under the title *Catch-18* in a literary quarterly that paid me twenty-five dollars, which wasn't too bad at the time. There was very little that wasn't too bad at the time.

"Then, in 1961," Joe continued, "in order to avoid a conflict with Leon Uris's *Mila 18*, my publisher, Simon & Schuster, said the title had to be changed. I thought about *Catch-11*, but then the movie *Ocean's Eleven* became popular. My editor, Bob Gottlieb, my agent, and I had been living with *Catch-18* for over five years, and the thought of changing it was a blow to us all.

"One morning that summer, Gottlieb called and said, 'I think I have it. Don't say no until you hear it: *Catch-22*.'

"'My God!' I said. 'That's it!'"

I've been privileged to know Joe and Valerie since that night in the hospital in 1981. I've even met their dog, Philippe, on a number of occasions. Joe, Speed, and Philippe, in the words of Larry L. King, have all been bugled to Jesus by now. Or Moses, as the case may be.

Valerie says Joe and Philippe were always great companions and, with their white, frizzy, curly hair, looked a lot alike. She also describes a trick that Joe taught Philippe. Joe would do this at the dinner parties no matter how fancy the occasion or how illustrious the guests.

"Up!" he would shout, at some point in the meal. And Philippe would jump into his lap and gobble up everything that was left on Joe's plate. When Philippe had finished licking the plate clean, Joe would shout, "Off!" and Philippe would jump down and bound happily on his way.

I once asked Joe Heller if he was happy. "What do you take me for," he said, "an idiot?"

"He's the wind beneath our wings."

DOM DELUISE, CHARLIE, BANJO, PAVAROTTI, *and* B. B.

LIKE JIM NABORS and Ruth Buzzi, Dom DeLuise has excelled in almost every aspect of show business, from stage to screen to television, from actor to singer to dancer to director, not to mention author and chef. From his first acting role as a kid as Bernie the Dog in *Bernie's Christmas Wish* to appearances with New York's Metropolitan Opera, to White House performances for four presidents, to his own successful television show, to countless motion pictures including half a dozen Mel Brooks movies, the most seminal of which was the iconic American classic *Blazing Saddles*, Dom has done it all.

So how do birds fit into Dom's life? Don't get your feathers ruffled, we're getting to that.

"I started out at the Cleveland Playhouse," Dom told me.

"I was alone and I wanted some company, so I got a bird. I've had them, or rather, they've had me ever since. I've lost some. A few flew away."

"How many birds do you have now?" I asked him.

"I have four birds, but I keep them in separate cages because their agents made me sign very strict contracts. Their names are Charlie, Banjo, Pavarotti, and B. B.

"Charlie does tricks. We have an act. Sometimes he swings by his beak from a stick, sometimes I pretend to eat him, and sometimes he acts like he's just had his way with a female eagle. The act took awhile to put together because originally I was the one who swung from a stick, but it was very hard for Charlie to hold on to the stick since he doesn't have opposable thumbs. I still get flowers from the female eagle, though."

"According to our mutual friend Kent Perkins," I said, "you often wear black shirts that become covered with bird shit on the shoulders. Is there any truth to this?"

"No, those are epaulets. But Charlie does go everywhere with me. Into the shower, under the covers. And sometimes we go to local schools to teach the kids compassion for animals."

"Where do you get these birds?"

"Two of the birds came to me from other homes. One had been abused. He won't tell me exactly what happened, only that he's no longer Catholic. The other ran away from a circus to join me. I think that's a compliment. The other bird I raised from an egg, which I had to explain to my wife, Carol. To this day she suspects that there was a bird that came between us, and the egg is partly mine. I tell her it's not true, but I still can't explain that time I came home with yolk on my collar.

"I treat my birds just like they're human. I talk to them, play with them, and give them attention. I love my birds and they love me back. And I'm still working on swinging from a stick."

"I'm telling you, it's all downhill from here."

ERNEST HEMINGWAY
and BLACK DOG

HEMINGWAY'S WRITING IS important for many reasons, not the least of which is that his style irritates many editors, charms many readers, and enlightens and influences many writers who like to break the rules. I long ago read an interview with the writer Dean Koontz who, at the time, was selling more books than McDonald's hamburgers and for all I know that may still be the case in some parallel universe. Koontz maintained that he was selling circles around Hemingway and Fitzgerald and that their work would soon disappear, having survived only by virtue of so many schools and universities making it required reading. My theory has always been that Dean Koontz would soon disappear. That hasn't happened either, but I'm currently rereading Hemingway's complete short stories (there are seventy-one) and recommend them highly.

I do not share Hemingway's famous love of bullfighting, deep-sea fishing, and big-game hunting, but human cruelty to animals has always been a hard cold truth, perhaps best elucidated in the fiction of Ernest Hemingway. At least he liked dogs and cats.

Indeed, Hemingway loved dogs and cats and horses, and who is to say that he did not also love bulls and marlins and elephants and lions, perhaps appreciating them in a primitive, almost primeval, adversarial manner, knowing that they might quite possibly be a method for sharpening his killing skills for that greatest, bloodiest, ultimately losing battle of them all, the one with himself.

Though Hemingway's famous six-toed cats still thrive in Key West, multiplying like the ancient Hebrews, it is a dog who, I believe, helped him the most to achieve the Nobel Prize for literature. The dog's name was Black Dog and he and his human counterpart were widely regarded as pretty far over the hill as they dedicated themselves to one last try for the brass ring of immortality. This was in Havana, where Hemingway had become a drinker with a writing problem and Black Dog was growing old and deaf.

Most of the literary world had written off Hemingway and Black Dog by this time. It had, after all, been a long time between dreams. In 1926, at the ripe old age of twenty-seven, with the publication of *The Sun Also Rises*, Hemingway had become immediately recognized as the leading writer of his time, the voice of "the lost generation." Now it had become a question of what have you done for us lately. Many critics felt that Hemingway had lost it.

The reason I include Black Dog in Hemingway's writing process is that both Hemingway and Black Dog did as well. Black Dog considered it his sacred duty to stay awake as Hemingway wrote feverishly through the night and then, when dawn had arrived and the night's work was done, the man and the dog would both crash together in a virtual state of exhaustion.

In 1954, Hemingway was awarded the Nobel Prize for *The Old Man and the Sea*, his last major work with Black Dog as his companion. While Hemingway was off the island, Black Dog, barely able to hear or see, attempted to protect the house from an intrusion by one of dictator Batista's goon squads. In the altercation, Black Dog was bludgeoned to death with a rifle butt. It could have been, as Hemingway himself believed, that receiving the Nobel Prize was the death knell to any great future work. It is also true that Hemingway was to write nothing of true spiritual substance after Black Dog was killed.

Hemingway committed suicide in 1961, at last, inevitably, bagging the biggest game of them all. As he crossed the Rainbow Bridge, Black Dog was waiting for him.

"We hear you've got some good grass."

WILLIE NELSON *and* A STABLE FULL OF HORSES

WILLIE NELSON, WHOM I call "the Hillbilly Dalai Lama," has often provided me with very sage advice over the many years I've known him. "If you're going to have sex with an animal," he told me recently, "always make it a horse. That way, if things don't work out, at least you know you've got a ride home."

This, as I often explain to the media, is a joke. And as Willie frequently observes, "Fuck 'em if they can't take a joke." When I say that Willie and I met on the gangplank of Noah's Ark, it is a particularly fitting commentary. And not just because, for the past few years, even with his incredibly busy schedule, Willie has somehow found the time to save a great many horses, most of whom, quite literally, had been at death's door.

About four years ago, during my campaign for governor of Texas (featuring Willie as my energy czar), we both began hearing reports about the horse slaughter plant in Kaufman, Texas, a small town thirty-five miles southeast of Dallas. The mayor of Kaufman, Paula Bacon, had been fighting to close the plant for years and, I believe, ultimately sacrificed her political career to save the horses.

According to Mayor Bacon, more than one hundred thousand horses were being killed annually by this plant, one in Ft. Worth and one in Illinois. These were not old and sick horses; many were young and healthy with the misfortune of having been sold to killer buyers. The three slaughter facilities shipped horsemeat to France and Belgium for table food. Willie and I both felt that this was not the cowboy way. That was how the campaign to "Save a Horse—Ride a Cowboy" began.

In November 2006, Willie, Paula Bacon, and I held a joint press conference to a sea of media at Willie's ranch outside Austin. Willie showed the press the twelve horses he'd saved from the slaughterhouse. They'd been in terrible shape when he'd adopted them a mere month earlier, but now they looked beautiful and were running freely about the ranch. Willie has now adopted fifty-one horses, including four colts born of the original twelve. His plan was to let people adopt the horses, but Willie has gotten so attached that he's decided to keep them all.

I told the media at that press conference that if I was elected governor, I would shut those slaughterhouses down. Unfortunately, the voters returned me to the private sector, but it was one campaign promise that I was able to keep. The slaughter plants in Kaufman and Ft. Worth have now been closed for good. Personally, I don't think it ever would've happened without the voice and the heart of Willie Nelson.

For more information, please go to Habitatforhorses.com.

"How many times do I have to tell you? I'm not a pit bull, I'm a Staffie!"

JIM NABORS, GYPSY, BARNEY, LULU, and DAISY

LIKE A SWALLOW, I return to Hawaii, often to Hilo, on the Big Island, where I trained for the Peace Corps in 1966, and to Honolulu, where I visit with old friends—one of whom happens to be Jim Nabors, a.k.a. Gomer Pyle. How did this unlikely friendship come about? Read on, gentile reader.

Long ago in a kingdom called the eighties, my friend Kent Perkins put an idea in my head. "As much as you go to Hawaii," he said, "you really ought to call Jim Nabors. He's been living there since the sixties. The nicest guy you'll ever meet. Look him up next time you go."

And so I did. It was almost surreal to find myself listening to that familiar Southern twang on the telephone. I kept waiting for him to say "Shazam!" Or maybe "Surprise!

Surprise! Surprise!" Sooner or later, he was bound to intone his iconic exclamation: "*Gohhhhhh-lee.*" But he said none of those things. Instead, he told me, "I'd love to show you my nuts." Only later did I learn that Jim had a macadamia plantation that took up about half of Maui.

When I finally met him the next day, I was startled by how much he looked like Gomer Pyle. Everybody else around us seemed to be doing double takes as well. It wasn't just old farts; young people too seemed to light up when they saw him. "That's why God created reruns," he said.

We had lunch at the New Otani Kaimana Beach Hotel on the lanai in the shadow of two big, gnarled interlocking hau trees under which, it is said, Robert Louis Stevenson first stayed when he visited Honolulu in 1889. There were no hotels on the island back then; room service was even slower than it is now.

Jim ordered sweetened tea, like he used to drink growing up. I ordered a piña colada, which is okay for a cowboy in Hawaii if you tell 'em to hold the umbrella.

Jim worked closely with just about every big star in the business, it seems, and counted Elvis, Frank, Dean, and Lucille Ball, to name only a few, among his dearest friends. His voice is a near operatic rich baritone, and he has recorded twenty-eight albums, a number of which have gone gold or platinum. But he's best known, of course, for his TV show *Gomer Pyle, U.S.M.C.,* a comedic but very human portrayal of the military that rose to prominence in the Vietnam era, at precisely the time the military was being vilified. Perhaps for that reason, Gomer Pyle is the only fictional character in history to receive a promotion in real life: to honorary lance corporal, by the commandant of the Marine Corps, James L. Jones, in 2001, and then to honorary corporal, by Lt. Gen. John F. Goodman, in 2007. To this day, drill instructors refer to recruits who need extra training as "gomers."

On my next trip to Honolulu, several years later, Jim invited me to his beautiful beachfront home, where I got to meet three of his friends: Richard Chamberlain, Liza Minnelli, and Andy Griffith. When Chamberlain learned I was from Texas, he gazed theatrically over the ocean and murmured in a voice worthy of *The Thorn Birds,* "Texas!" I also met Daisy, Lulu, Gypsy, and Barney, Jim's four six-year-old Staffordshire terriers. "They're the smartest, sweetest, most loyal dogs you'll ever see," he said. "They're just like people; they need to be raised with love." And so they are. Every July 3rd, in what has become a sort of pilgrimage, Jim and his pilot, Stan, load up Daisy, Lulu, Gypsy, and Barney into his twin-engine plane and fly them over to Maui. The reason? "They are frightened by the fireworks," says Jim.

On that same trip, Jim told me a story about a conversation he had had while he was waiting to meet the Queen at Buckingham Palace. A man with a big mustache, a monocle, and a large colorful sash across his tuxedo walked up to

him and said, "Pity about the Wales." The man was refer-
ring to the imminent breakup of Princess Diana and Prince
Charles. Jim, however, thought he was talking about the
Japanese killing whales off Hawaii. "I like to watch them," he
said. "I've even seen them mate a few times." That was the
only time he ever witnessed a monocle actually pop out of
someone's eye.

My most recent trip to Hawaii was in February, and of
course I saw Jim, who's now seventy-nine. He told me a story
that I took home as a gift. It was 1964 and *Gomer Pyle*, in its
first year, was already one of the hottest shows going. Someone came up to Jim on the set one day and asked, "Have you
heard of Cassius Clay?" Jim said, "Yeah. The boxer." The guy
said, "Well, his mother and his little brother are here, and
they're huge fans of yours. Do you have time to say hello to
them?"

Jim said, "Sure." He went over and met them and took
pictures and signed autographs, and he kind of liked Clay's
mother. She was a down-home sort of woman from Ken-
tucky, and Jim himself is from Alabama, so he invited the
two of them to have lunch with him in the commissary.
Lots of stars came and went, and Jim introduced them all
to Clay's mother and little brother. Afterward, they hugged
and said good-bye, and Jim never saw them again.

Twenty-five years later, Jim was having dinner with
Carol Burnett at Le Dome, in Los Angeles, when a big party

of people came in. The buzz was that it was Muhammad Ali and his entourage. Jim just continued with his dinner— he had never spoken to or met Ali, and he didn't want to bother him. Also, rumors had been circulating that Ali had lost his memory from two and a half decades in the ring.

About halfway through the meal, Jim felt a tap on his shoulder. When he looked up, Ali was standing over him. Ali leaned down and said, "Thanks for being so nice to my mama and my little brother."

That story shows just how long an act of kindness can float around in the universe. It also shows how a nice guy can sometimes finish first. Aloha, Gomer. Until we meet again.

"Are you sure you're a Democrat?"

MY PET PROJECT

TO THOSE OF you who think my career is going to the dogs, I say, "You're right." It's also going to the cats. Because they need my help. Yours too.

It's true, folks. I'm known far and wide as the Gandhi-like figure of the Utopia Animal Rescue Ranch. What, you might ask, does a Gandhi-like figure do? Nothing, of course. And what kind of profit does this modern-day prophet earn from the daunting task of doing nothing all the time? None, of course. But if you keep asking questions, you're going to irritate the Gandhi-like figure, who has his hands full as the spiritual leader of sixty-three dogs, twenty-two horses, three donkeys, nine pigs, two goats, eleven cats, fifteen chickens, two turkeys, and a rooster named Alfred Hitchcock who crows precisely at noon.

It all started one morning late in the summer of 1996 at the ungodly hour of seven o'clock as my dog Mr. Magoo and I were driving the campers' dirty laundry into Kerrville from my family's summer camp, Echo Hill. Some might find it rather sad that, after fifty years of camping, my role had devolved to this pathetic, menial task. To me and Magoo, however, this was an important mission, fraught with many obstacles and challenges, one of which we spotted in the middle of the road that very morning. I slammed on the brakes of the old pickup, leaped sideways out of the cab, and discovered a kitten nestled between the yellow stripes of the highway, roaring like a tiger. The pitiable creature, all of five inches long, was bleeding profusely from a gaping wound in his right front leg.

Certain that the animal was dying, Magoo and I scooped him up and raced him to our friend Bill Hoegemeyer's animal clinic in Kerrville. Dr. Hoegemeyer's diagnosis was that the little fellow had been shot by some great white hunter. I told him to do whatever it took to save the cat. He amputated the leg, gave the patient two injections during surgery to restart his heart, then gave me a bill for $1,200. I didn't know it then, but Lucky—for that was to become the cat's name—would have a worth that would be virtually incalculable.

In a short period of time, I realized that I'd be on the road too much to provide adequately for the care and feeding of the little convalescing feline patient. So I, for want of a better word, dumped him on Cousin Nancy Parker, a friend of mine who lived in Utopia. In all fairness, Lucky was not the first, nor would he be the last, furry soul I was to deposit on Cousin Nancy's doorstep. I have always felt that what we do when a stray spirit crosses our path—how we react to the hungry, homeless stranger—is indubitably a measure of our own humanity.

In time, Cousin Nancy's little menagerie grew. Soon she had so many animals that she didn't know what to do. Because of this, in 1998 the Utopia Animal Rescue Ranch was born. It was and still is a never-kill sanctuary for stray and abused animals, a court of last resort for those at death's door. But playing God is a role with which Cousin Nancy and I have never felt comfortable. We always knew we could not save every starfish on the sand, only this one.

Today, as before, Cousin Nancy runs the show; her husband, Tony Simons (who can identify each dog by his or her individual bark), is our ranch manager; and I suppose I fall into the category of modern-day Ronald Reagan pitchman. Nearly seven years ago, my father, Tom Friedman, in the last year of his life, provided the Rescue Ranch with a new home on the scenic east flat of Echo Hill. Here the animals, in spacious outdoor pens, are cared for by Nancy and Tony, sheltered by the surrounding hills, and protected from a world that, at best, has never been very kind to them. The zip code is Medina, but the ranch is still Utopia. More than anything else, it feels like a peaceful, happy orphanage.

During the eleven years of the ranch's existence, many friends and angels have come to our rescue, just as the ranch has come to the rescue of so many animals in distress. My friend John McCall, the Shampoo King from Dripping Springs, and many others have made large financial contributions. Dwight Yoakam, Jerry Jeff Walker, Billy Joe Shaver, Robert Earl Keen, Steven Fromholz, the Flatlanders, and too many other great musicians to name have headlined "Bonefits" to raise more money. Jerry Agiewich has distributed a line of salsas that has similarly been a financial pleasure. Former First Lady Laura Bush graciously sponsored a luncheon for us at the Four Seasons in Austin. Artist Peter Max donated a portrait of the Kinkster with two of the Friedmans, Brownie and Chumley. And Cousin Nancy has written a book about our adventures titled *The Road to Utopia: How Kinky, Tony & I Saved More Animals Than Noah* (published by the University of Texas Press).

What can you do to help? Consider adopting an animal. More than two thousand Rescue Ranch residents have already been welcomed into loving homes all over the country. (To see photos of the animals up for adoption, go to utopia rescue.com.) Taking in a stray or abused animal can be a life-changing experience, but don't be surprised if your new pet gazes wistfully over his shoulder as you both drive away. Utopia is quite possibly the only real home he's ever known. If you watch carefully, you might even see Cousin Nancy cry.

Of course, she'll always have Lucky. The three-legged cat shares Cousin Nancy and Tony's trailer on the Rescue Ranch with twelve dogs whom he routinely keeps in line with the mere swat of a paw. With the same solitary front paw, he has killed two rattlesnakes. He is, indeed, a very lucky cat. Strong, handsome, and high-spirited, he is a living symbol of what a little love can do.

I've always believed that dogs are cowboys and cats are Indians, natural enemies fighting forever across the wide-open prairie of the imagination of a child. Taken together, however, they could well constitute the yin and the yang of our souls. It wouldn't even rain very hard if it weren't for cats and dogs. Their only fault is that they never live long enough.

Mark Twain once said that when you meet Saint Peter, it's best to leave your dog outside. Heaven, he claimed, runs on protocol. If it ran on merit, your dog would go in and you would stay outside.

As usual, Mark Twain was not wrong. It's just another reason why I always say that money may buy you a fine dog, but only love can make him wag his tail.

"We're going to Texas?"

KINKY and CUDDLES

O N JANUARY 4, 1993, the cat in this book and the books that preceded it was put to sleep in Kerrville, Texas, by Dr. W. H. Hoegemeyer and myself. Cuddles was fourteen years old, a respectable age. She was as close to me as any human being I have ever known.

Cuddles and I spent many years together, both in New York, where I first found her as a little kitten on the street in Chinatown, and later on the ranch in Texas. She was always with me, on the table, on the bed, by the fireplace, beside the typewriter, on top of my suitcase when I returned from a trip.

I dug Cuddles's grave with a silver spade in the little garden by the stream behind the old green trailer where both of us lived in the summertime. Her burial shroud was my old New York sweatshirt and in the grave with her is a can of tuna and a cigar.

A few days after Cuddles crossed the Rainbow Bridge, I received a sympathy note from Bill Hoegemeyer, the veterinarian. It opened with a verse by Irving Townsend: "We who choose to surround ourselves with lives even more temporary than our own live within a fragile circle."

Now, as I write this, on a gray winter day by the fireside, I can almost feel her light tread, moving from my head and my heart down through my fingertips to the keys of the typewriter. People may surprise you with unexpected kindness. Dogs have a depth of loyalty that often we seem unworthy of. But the love of a cat is a blessing, a privilege in this world.

They say when you die and go to heaven all the dogs and cats you've ever had in your life come running to meet you.

Until that day, rest in peace, Cuddles.

JOHN CALLAHAN and STANLEY

JOHN CALLAHAN IS a longtime friend of mine whose art has often gotten him in a lot of trouble. He's pissed off Christians, Catholics, Jews, African Americans, Asians, Hispanics, Native Americans, pro-choice activists, animal lovers, women in general, people who suffer from bulimia, people who suffer from anorexia, people who suffer from Tourette's syndrome, people who suffer from every disability imaginable, and mainly people who suffer from the most pernicious disease known to mankind: the lack of a sense of humor.

Callahan's cartoons, invariably and unerringly stabbing the senses with truth, honesty, spiritual integrity (as well as being funny as hell), have appeared in hundreds of newspapers and magazines, and were published in fourteen of his own books. His work has also graced the pages of several of my books, including *Texas Hold 'Em* and *What Would*

Kinky Do? As well as being the brains behind several television series, and having his autobiography optioned by William Hurt, Robin Williams, and Showtime, Callahan is now the subject of a new film by the Dutch documentary filmmaker Simone DeVries. It is titled *Touch Me Someplace I Can Feel.*

John Callahan also writes songs. Two years ago, at the ripe young age of fifty-three, he released his first CD to raves from the critics and the multitudes in the musical community who'd had their hip cards punched. The CD, *Purple Winos in the Rain,* contains some of the best songs I've heard since Christ was a cowboy.

Callahan comes as close as anyone I know to personifying my definition of an artist: someone who's ahead of his time and behind on his rent. While this is perhaps only half true in Callahan's case, there are, it appears, a few minor extenuating circumstances. John, for most of his adult life, has been a much-celebrated, much vilified paralyzed genius.

"What I like about being paralyzed," he says, "is that it's so utterly limiting that it's also liberating."

Perhaps you are wondering, with the condition his condition is in, how can Callahan draw cartoons at all? Well, from what I understand, it ain't easy. I'll let him describe the process in his own words: "I clutch the pen between both hands in a pathetic, childlike manner that somehow endears me to millions of conflicted fans around the world."

"I think you're better looking than Elton John."

Callahan does not live what some might call a normal existence, but who worth a shit ever really does? I strongly recommend, gentile reader, that you check out John Callahan the Cartoonist on MySpace since John can't remember what his own website is. Like me, he doesn't have a computer, doesn't have e-mail, and his favorite TV show is still *Bonanza.*

Many animals have come into and gone out of John Callahan's life. Indeed, several of his cartoon collections have been devoted exclusively to dogs and cats. One of my favorites is a dog walking down a sidewalk with a donkey standing on its back, and a construction worker saying, "Look at the ass on that bitch!"

The cat in this photograph is named Stanley, who died in 2006 at the age of seventeen. Stanley had tremendous charisma and was well known in the neighborhood for swaggering in through other people's cat doors and eating their cat's food or their own food off the breakfast table. Unfortunately, Stanley was a serial killer of birds, rodents, and anything smaller than him. He considered the neighbor's birdbath his lazy Susan. Stanley would often scratch John's legs rather severely. "Fortunately," says Callahan, "I couldn't feel it."

Callahan has had several other pets in his recent life. One of them was Snickers. "Snickers was a golden mini-weeney dog," he says, "about the size of a baguette." John, who lives in Portland where it rains all the time, when not watching *Bonanza* has spent an inordinate amount of time watching *Perry Mason*.

"It was uncanny," he says. "Every time Paul Drake, Perry Mason's private investigator, would come on the screen, Snickers would bark uncontrollably at the sound of his voice."

Callahan also had an African gray parrot named Festus, whom he took on book tours with him for a while, but Festus bit people hard and often, so this practice had to be discontinued. Festus's cage was located next to a sliding glass door that made a hideous scraping sound every time it was opened or closed. He mimicked that sound, and only that sound, perfectly. Callahan eventually gave Festus to his girlfriend, who later died. He assures me, however, that Festus is still living in East Portland. Callahan, who is a dealer in hope and has inspired many people, takes some little comfort in knowing that Festus will be there, still impersonating that sliding glass door, long after all the rest of us are gone.

"Your place or mynah?"

BILLY BOB THORNTON *and* ALICE

THE WORD "ECCENTRIC" is something of an understatement when you're talking about Billy Bob Thornton. I met him for the first time years ago in Hollywood. He was introduced to me by the great country singer Dwight Yoakam. Dwight has never smoked or drunk alcohol in his entire life and he is an extremely meticulous vegetarian. Billy Bob, "Billy" to his intimates, suffers from none of Dwight's afflictions. He chain-smokes, has been known to drink an adult portion of alcohol, and eats an appropriate amount for his figure, which he always keeps just slightly skinnier than the scarecrow in the *Wizard of Oz*.

Since my first meeting with Billy, I've shared meals with him, been to his home, hung out with him onstage, offstage, backstage, and on the occasional movie set. He clearly suffers from the curse of being multitalented. He is a superb actor. He also writes music and lyrics that I personally compare favorably with the likes of Leonard Cohen, though I don't think Billy gets enough credit for it. Of course, when *Forbes* magazine estimates your earnings last year at $20 million, perhaps you don't really care how seriously critics regard your music. After all, he is a rare, not to say strange, bird. Perhaps that's why Billy's into birds.

The reader will note that throughout these files, *only* Billy Bob Thornton and Dom DeLuise freely admit to being bird people. What does this signify? What does this tell us? Not a fucking thing, I'm afraid. Both men are fine actors. One is very thin and one is, shall we say, rather plump. Both are highly talented musically. Did the birds teach them or did they teach the birds? We would require Maya Angelou and a phalanx of shrinks to resolve this existential question, and it's a lot more fun to hang out with Billy Bob or Dom than it is to hang out with Maya Angelou and a phalanx of shrinks.

Over the years, I have observed several of Billy's unconventional behaviors. One is that when he's busy chain smoking his American Spirit cigarettes in the yellow box, he always places three of them exactly symmetrically on top of the box. He is exceedingly careful never to point the lit end of a cigarette directly at anyone because he believes it will make them die. Doctors, of course, believe that smoking cigarettes will make him die. But I believe there are more old birds than there are old doctors.

Billy, since childhood, had always wanted a mynah bird, and now he has one. Her name is Alice. She hates women, according to Billy, but is soothed somewhat by Captain Beefheart's poetry, which he leaves on every time he goes away from the house. Billy told me, "I'm the only person who can put his hand in the cage without being clawed to pieces." According to Billy, "Alice talks a lot. She tries to say, 'Fuck you,' but always has a little trouble with it. She does better with, 'I wish you'd leave.' Alice is the real lunatic in this house."

Billy does have a few quirks of his own. For instance, he has a fear of antique furniture, a phobia shared by the Dwight Yoakam character in the Thornton-penned classic, *Sling Blade*. He also has a fear of certain types of flatware. "It's just that I won't use real silver," he says, "like those big old heavy-ass forks and knives. I can't do that. It's the same as the antique furniture. I just don't like old stuff. I'm creeped out by it and I don't know why. I don't have a phobia about American antiques, it's mostly French—you know, like the big old gold-carved chairs with the velvet cushions."

Antiques are not the only things that freak Billy out; he's phobic about dust, castles, germs, Komodo dragons, clowns, flying, and harpsichords. There's nothing wrong with that, I always tell him. That's perfectly normal.

Other than Alice, Billy has had many animals in the past: dogs, cats, and a pet rat named Fat Harry who used to sleep in his own hammock when Billy lived with Angelina. He does have a phobia about reptiles, however. When he bought his current house from Slash (Guns N' Roses bass player and lead man of Velvet Revolver), he did not know that Slash had kept his pet boa constrictor in the house. This required Billy's hiring a professional snake handler to comb the place for snake eggs and/or baby boas. When the all clear was given, Billy and Alice moved in.

STRANGE BEDFELLOWS

PERHAPS YOU ARE wondering what some of my own pets are like. What follows is a typical night living with the Friedmans at the ranch.

I sleep in an old ranch house in the Hill Country with a shotgun under my bed and a cat on my head. The cat's name is Lady Argyle, and she used to belong to my mother before Mom stepped on a rainbow. It is not a pleasant situation when you have a cat who insists on sleeping on your head like a hat and putting her whiskers in your left nostril all night long at intervals of about twenty-seven minutes. I haven't actually timed this behavioral pattern, but it wouldn't surprise me if the intervals were precisely twenty-seven minutes. This precarious set of affairs could have easily resulted in a hostage situation or a suicide pact, but as of this writing, neither has occurred. The two reasons are that I love Lady as much as a man is capable of loving a cat and

Lady loves me as much as a cat is capable of loving a man. It is a blessing when an independent spirit like a cat loves you, and it's a common human failing to underestimate or trivialize such a bond. On the other hand, it's not a healthy thing to observe a man going to bed with a cat on his head like a hat. And, in the case of Lady and myself, there *are* observers.

The observers of this van Gogh mental hospital scenario are four dogs, all of whom despise Lady—though not half as much as Lady despises them. The dogs sleep on the bed too, and they find it unnerving, not to say unpleasant, to be in the presence of a man who has a cat on his head. I've tried to discuss this with them on innumerable occasions, but it isn't easy to state your case to four dogs who are looking at you with pity in their eyes.

Mr. Magoo is five years old and highly skilled at being resigned to a sorry situation. He's a deadbeat dad, so his two sons, Brownie and Chumley, are with us as well. Brownie and Chumley were named after my sister Marcie's two imaginary childhood friends and fairly recently have been left in my care, as she departed for Vietnam with the International Red Cross, an assignment she correctly deduced might be harmful to the health, education, and welfare of Brownie and Chumley. The animals divide their time between my place and the Utopia Animal Rescue Ranch, a sanctuary for abused and stray animals.

"Settle down, fellas, it's only *60 Minutes*."

If you were spiritually deprived as a child and are not an animal lover, you may already be in a coma from reading this. That's good because I don't care a flea about people who don't love animals. I shall continue my impassioned tale, and I shall not stop until the last dog is sleeping.

The last dog is Hank. He looks like one of the flying monkeys in *The Wizard of Oz*, and he doesn't understand that the cat can and will hurt him and me and the entire Polish army if we get in her way. Lady is about eighteen years old and has lived in this house on this ranch almost all her life, and she doesn't need to be growled at by a little dog with a death wish.

So I've got the cat hanging down over one side of my face like a purring stalactite with her whiskers poking into my left nostril and Hank on the other side who completely fails to grasp the mortal danger he's placing both of us in by playfully provoking the cat. It's 3:09 in the morning, and suddenly a deafening cacophony of barking, hissing, and shrieking erupts, with Lady taking a murderous swat at Hank directly across my fluttering eyelids and Mr. Magoo stepping heavily on my slumbering scrotum as all of the animals bolt off the bed simultaneously. This invariably signals the arrival of Dilly, my pet armadillo.

Dilly has been showing up with the punctuality of a German train in my backyard for years. I feed him cat food, dog food, bacon grease, anything. He is a shy, crepuscular, oddly

Christ-like creature whose arrival brings a measure of comfort to me at the same time it causes all of the dogs to go into attack mode. It is not necessary to describe what effect this always has on Lady.

After I've slipped outside and fed Dilly, I gather the animals about me like little pieces of my soul. I explain to them once again that Dilly is an old, spiritual friend of mine who is cursed with living in a state full of loud, brash Texans, and we don't have to make things worse. Somewhere there is a planet, I tell them, inhabited principally by sentient armadillos who occasionally carve up dead humans and sell them as baskets by the roadside. Perhaps not surprisingly, the animals seem to relate to this peculiar vision. Then we all go back to bed and dream of fields full of slow-moving rabbits and mice and cowboys and Indians and imaginary childhood friends and tail fins on Cadillacs and girls in the summertime and everything else that time has taken away.

All the saints rejoice in heaven, when the fallen angels fly.
—Billy Joe Shaver

EMMYLOU HARRIS, KEETA, and BELLA

IN 1973, AS I was touring with my first album, *Sold American*, one of my true heroes went to Jesus. Gram Parsons was only twenty-six years old, but his death was like a modern-day Hank Williams experience to me. I liked him not only for his imagination, style, and spiritual integrity, but I also felt he represented in one person the best that country music had been and a new, exciting direction for what it could be. This is why, perhaps, I've sometimes been quoted as saying, "I'd rather be a dead Gram Parsons than a live Garth Brooks."

I never got to meet Gram, but I've gotten to know someone who was closer to him than anybody, who harmonized perfectly with him in every way, and who has kept his spirit alive in the fickle, often fallow fields of country music. Her name, of course, is Emmylou Harris, and I've been delighted to see that someone so talented and so kind-hearted has been able not only to survive but to thrive in the wicked world we sometimes call the music business. Perhaps she has an angel on her shoulder.

Emmylou has won twelve Grammys and three CMA awards, and was named the fifth greatest woman of all time in country music (and the other four had better watch out because she ain't done yet!). This remarkable record of success is rendered even more amazing when you stop to consider that Emmylou has never followed the proven, formulaic, conventional paths to commercial success. She is a genre-transcending experimenter, perhaps a visionary, who may show up playing old-timey country, rock, acoustic, or solo performances, and feeling equally comfortable with each.

Another reason I find Emmylou admirable and inspiring is that someone so busy with writing, recording, sound tracks, concert tours, etc., still finds time to do so much good in the world. Whether it's Concerts for a Landmine Free World, or promoting feminism in music, or boycotting KFC for PETA, or saving the old historic Ryman Auditorium in Nashville, or helping hurricane victims with events like Shelter from the Storm: A Concert for the Gulf Coast, Emmylou has been there to lend her voice and her heart.

"I don't do music videos," she says, "but I do animal videos." Emmylou not only sponsors a pen at Utopia Animal Rescue Ranch, but she's also given generously to every animal rescue group under the sun including the Humane Society of the United States, Best Friends, PETA, many local groups in Tennessee, and her own little shelter in her backyard called Bonaparte's Retreat. It is named for a poodle mix named Bonaparte who toured with Emmylou, was one of her closest friends, and crossed the Rainbow Bridge at the respectable old age of fifteen.

Bonaparte's Retreat is a fostering operation that specializes in the dogs who are the hardest to place—those who are older, have been relinquished more than once, or have been available for adoption for a long time. Emmylou says, "I feel the sorriest for those who've been there the longest and languish in cages and runs. I try to socialize them and just give 'em love." With Bonaparte's Retreat, Emmylou has turned her own backyard into a shelter and animal sanctuary, complete with runs and doghouses. Some of her current guests can be seen on her website, www.emmylou.net.

"Animals can teach us how to be better human beings," Emmylou says. "My dogs are both rescues. Keeta [German shepherd mix on the left] is my 'road dog'. She was displaced by a hurricane in 2005 but now travels comfortably with me on tour. Bella [on the right] is a Lab mix from Metro Animal Control in Nashville, where she was next in line to be euthanized. But really, they rescued me. It can be a lonely life out there on the road, and there's no better company than a dog (or two!). They love the bus, they love the hotels, they love the venues, they love the people. But most of all, they love you."

"Great, he forgot his pants again."

CLIVE CUSSLER and BUSTER

CLIVE CUSSLER HAS long been one of my literary heroes, though in my opinion, the literary critics have rarely given him the respect he richly deserves. Come to think of it, if they had, he probably wouldn't have been one of my heroes. The critics didn't much respect the great mystery writer Raymond Chandler either. He's the one who once wrote, "The business of fiction is to re-create the illusion of life." That is part of the reason Clive Cussler has a readership of more than 125 million people around the world. It's also part of the reason you never see a statue of a critic.

Fiction is sometimes, I believe, the best truth we have. Clive Cussler has published more than forty books in more than forty languages in more than a hundred countries, and, though the books are fiction, their historical accuracy remains unimpeached and unsurpassed. They are adventure stories that entertain as well as educate the reader, much like the works of Robert Louis Stevenson.

Cussler began writing in 1965 when his wife took a night job with the local police department where they lived in California. After cooking dinner for the kids and putting them to bed, Cussler says, he had no one to talk to and nothing to do, so he started writing. The character he created was a marine engineer, government agent, and adventurer named Dirk Pitt. Dirk Pitt has always been extremely popular with readers, including myself.

And yes, Virginia, there really is a NUMA (National Underwater and Marine Agency). It's a nonprofit group started by Cussler that has located more than sixty shipwrecks of historical significance. Among these are the long-lost Confederate submarine the CSS *Hunley*, perhaps best known as the first submarine to sink a ship in battle, and the ship it sank, the *Housatonic*; the *U-20*, the U-boat that sank the *Lusitania*; the Republic of Texas Navy warship *Zavala*, found under a parking lot in Galveston, Texas; and the wreck of the *Carpathia*, the valiant vessel that navigated icebergs in order to rescue the survivors of the *Titanic*.

Clive Cussler had two childhood dogs of note. One was Buster. "Buster was a mutt," he says. "He was old when my uncle gave him to me. But he was a lovable dog. He preferred eating fish over meat.

"The dachshund was Schnapps. Now there was a character. When I was young I played the violin. When other kids had lemonade stands I used to take Schnapps to a busy street corner and play my violin. I guess high notes hurt his ears and he used to sit up, wave his front paws, and howl up a storm. It was almost as if he was singing along. People were so amused that one day I believe we cleared eighty cents, which was quite good considering it was the Depression."

"I'm not really high maintenance."

BRIAN WILSON and SARAH

BRIAN WILSON'S MUSIC is the secret poetry of the innocence that we lose as we grow up. Part of Brian's charm and eccentric nature, ironically, is the fact that he has not grown up; he's only gotten older. And, as millions around the world can attest, he always was a veteran soul.

At the age of nineteen, he recorded "Surfin'" in his parents' living room with his younger brothers Dennis and Carl, his cousin Mike, and friend Al Jardine. This was destined to become the very first single for the band that was destined to become the Beach Boys.

Three albums later, Brian took over the role of the band's producer, and seven albums followed in rapid succession. Many of the songs dealt with—what else?—surfing. This was mildly ironic because Brian himself was phobic about going into the water. But the themes of the songs were soon to broaden and, of course, to deepen.

Brian retired from touring with the Beach Boys in 1964, devoting all his considerable energy to writing and producing for the band. Two years later, at the age of twenty-four, Brian wrote what many have called "the greatest album of all time," *Pet Sounds*. It is no spiritual stretch to say this work made him one of the most important composers of the last century, guaranteeing him the best table at any restaurant, except that he never went out.

"Danny Hutton may have introduced me to Brian," says my friend Van Dyke Parks. "I knew a lot of people who knew Brian Wilson. The first piece I got to hear from Brian was when I went up to his house with David Crosby, who's also said he introduced me to Brian. The first thing he played us on a four-track was the basic track to *Sloop John B. Sloop John B.*, of course, was a folk song, which indicated we'd been somewhat influenced by the same things and I thought it spoke very highly of him as well as his nod to folk music at that moment. He had great curiosity; he was a man of inquiry, with a discerning mind and a good heart. Even at the age of twenty-two, I saw he was a person of great consequence."

In creating *Pet Sounds*, the twenty-four-year-old composer, arranger, and producer broke all conventional rules of recording. Indeed, Paul McCartney picks it as his favorite album, claiming that *Sgt. Pepper* never would've happened without *Pet Sounds*. According to Beatles producer George

Martin, "*Pepper* was an attempt to equal *Pet Sounds*." And Bob Dylan claims, "Brian Wilson made all his records with four tracks, but you couldn't make his records if you had a hundred tracks today." Brian and the Beach Boys were inducted into the Rock and Roll Hall of Fame in January 1988, alongside the Beatles and Dylan.

Brian Wilson, by all accounts a gentle giant, has always had animals around him, some even of the two-legged variety. On *Pet Sounds*, he closes the poignant song "Caroline, No" with the sounds of an onrushing train and the barking of Banana and Louie, his two dogs at the time. He now is said to have twenty-one miniature dogs, who all live in his kitchen. Multiple sources assure me this is true, and if indeed it is, my respect for him is even greater.

Brian's wife, Melinda, says that the Maltese in the photograph with Brian is named Sarah. "Sarah is an eight-year-old California Girl," says Melinda, "who is in love with Brian Wilson and her princess pink food bowl, not necessarily in that order. She became a Brian Wilson fan at the ripe old age of ten weeks when she moved in with him and was given her all-access pass. Her favorite CD is *Pet Sounds* and she especially relates to the last track, 'Caroline, No.' Sarah loves the ocean and has a hot pink bikini with sunglasses and visor to match. You can take the bitch off of the beach, but you can't take the beach away from the bitch."

"This is where he got the idea for *Blazing Saddles*."

RICHARD PRYOR and GINGER

I T IS NOT surprising that Richard Pryor became a comedian. Without the ability to laugh at himself, his life, and the whole world, he never would've survived. Pryor's life is an incredible rags-to-riches story, but as is so often the case, it was the rags that made him who he was.

Born into poverty in Illinois, raised in his grandmother's brothel after being abandoned by his mother, raped at six by a teenage neighbor, and molested later by a Catholic priest, he watched his mother perform sex acts upon the mayor of Peoria. He was expelled from school at age fourteen and got his first real job, working as a janitor at a local strip club. It is remarkable that he came to be regarded by those who knew him as a man with no self-pity.

Inspired by Bill Cosby, he played in clubs in New York and opened for Bobby Darin in Vegas, where he soon found the format too constraining. Though he made more than fifty movies, most of which he considered typical formulaic Hollywood crap, he created many more black pearls of comic genius than he may have realized.

His first screenwriting attempt was *Blazing Saddles* with Mel Brooks, which garnered him the Writers Guild of America Award for Best Comedy Written Directly for the Screen. He also had a big hand in writing *Sanford and Son*, *The Flip Wilson Show*, and two Lily Tomlin specials, one of which earned him an Emmy and a Writers Guild award.

But Richard Pryor was probably best loved for being an observer of life in that sacred casino of truth, live comedy. In my opinion, almost no one has performed this mission of magic messenger better. He had the God-given ability to make a cosmic joke out of cocaine addiction, eight marriages, two heart attacks and quadruple bypass surgery, killing his car, multiple sclerosis, a childhood from hell, and last, but not least, the famous incident of setting himself on fire, resulting in third-degree burns over fifty percent of his body. Now that's talent!

Aside from being an enduring cultural icon, Richard Pryor had a longtime, deep, abiding love for all animals. Until his death in 2005, he lived with his two rescued dogs, Homer and Spirit. He and his wife, Jennifer Lee, have been friends and generous supporters of Utopia Animal Rescue Ranch. After his death, Jennifer Lee started a nonprofit in his honor called Pryor's Planet, an organization dedicated to helping grassroots efforts in saving the lives of animals, providing sanctuary, and making the world a better place for all creatures.

Ginger the miniature horse was a gift from the producer Burt Sugarman when Richard was doing *The Richard Pryor Comedy Show.* Richard told the story of his Great Dane trying repeatedly to mount Ginger and used the bit later in his concert film *Wanted: Richard Pryor, Live in Concert.*

Richard, according to Jennifer Lee, loved to take Ginger for walks in his Northridge Estate Orange Grove. At the end of the walk, she says, Richard and Ginger would always eat oranges together.

In 2000, as the Ringling Bros. and Barnum & Bailey circus was preparing to open at Madison Square Garden, Richard Pryor wrote a letter to the Big Top's first African-American ringmaster, Jonathan Lee Iverson. "While I am hardly one to complain about a young African American making an honest living," he wrote, "I urge you to ask yourself just how honorable it is to preside over the abuse and suffering of animals."

"Yes, he really believes he's a dog."

DANNY HUTTON, MISSY, *and* BUDDY—
A THREE DOG NIGHT

THE GREAT IRISH writer Brendan Behan once wrote, "Other people have a nationality, the Irish and Jews have a psychosis." Perhaps that's why Danny Hutton and I have felt like blood brothers for all these years. He was born in Ireland and I'm a hebe from the heart of Texas. For whatever the reason, Danny and I are alive and well at this writing, and many of the people we once knew are now dead or wishing they were. Perhaps the two of us have been blessed and the Lord is working through us to reach others? No, that couldn't be it.

Danny Hutton, the brains, driving spiritual force, and one of the three lead singers in Three Dog Night, has had a huge impact on music and the music business, not to mention, he lived to tell the story. Between 1969 and 1975, Three

Dog Night sold more than fifty million albums, a feat that no American vocal group had ever accomplished.

Danny Hutton and Three Dog Night lived in the fast lane and recorded and toured at an incredibly brutal pace. "To give you an idea of just how fast the pace was back then," he says, "the first album was completed in a matter of days." Their manager had barely gotten over the name of the band. "Why do you want to call yourselves dogs?" the manager wondered. "That's a horrible name!" But the hits kept comin'.

With the vocal harmonies of Danny, Cory Wells, and Chuck Negron, Three Dog Night unleashed twenty-one hit singles and thirteen gold albums. Danny's "triadic" approach to reinforced trio arrangements became the signature for many groups that followed, including the Beatles beginning with *Help!*, Crosby, Stills & Nash, the Eagles, and a slew of folk-rock-country crossover and pop groups. Brian Wilson was reportedly fascinated with Danny's early studio innovations and recognized him as an equal. Danny had a desire to "create character" with each voice, "to create someone who'd never existed, to put someone out there in the ether."

The songs, of course, all handpicked with the Hutton touch, became practically part of the fabric of the times. They were the first megahits for the songwriters as well. "One (Is the Loneliest Number)" by Harry Nilsson. "Mama Told Me Not to Come" by Randy Newman. "Joy to the World" by Hoyt Axton. "Old Fashioned Love Song" by Paul

Williams. "Shambala" by B. W. Stevenson. "Eli's Comin'" by Laura Nyro. "The Show Must Go On" by Leo Sayer. "Never Been to Spain" (Hoyt Axton again), "Liar," "Sure as I'm Sittin' Here," "Black and White," etc., etc.

Derek Taylor was Danny's publicist as well as publicist for the Beatles. He claims that when the Beatles saw Danny's promo shots with his new mustache, they all thought it looked so great they decided to sport mustaches just like Danny's. And then there was the young British guy named Reggie Dwight who pitched two songs to Danny, both of which Three Dog Night subsequently recorded. Reggie Dwight's first song was called "Lady Samantha." The second one was "Your Song," and Three Dog's version catapulted Reggie, by then known as Elton John, to international fame. Elton John later recorded what is widely regarded as a tribute song to the man who'd helped him. It was called "Daniel."

Danny now has a wife and children and dogs of his own. Danny's wife, Laurie, says that Missy is a one-hundred-pound Labradoodle, given to Danny by Brian Wilson and his wife, Melinda. "Missy's mother was a big, fat, blond Lab," says Laurie, "and her father was a tall, handsome standard poodle."

There is a long story about how Buddy wound up with the Huttons. In order to prevent the reader from developing ennui, I'll give you the short version: Lady gets Buddy from the pound. Buddy doesn't like lady, escapes to Huttons. Laurie loves Buddy but Danny thinks he looks too much like a coyote because he's so skinny. Lady comes over, wants Buddy back. Takes Buddy away, Laurie heartbroken. Buddy escapes again, goes back to Huttons. Too skinny, says Danny, looks like a coyote. Buddy goes, says Danny. Buddy stays, says Laurie. Lady comes back, says Buddy can stay with Huttons. Danny says okay, if Laurie cooks Buddy people food so he doesn't look like coyote.

So here they are together on the Chinese wedding bed. Missy, Danny, and Buddy—just another Three Dog Night. I say, long may they run.

VAN DYKE PARKS *and* JUBAL

VAN DYKE PARKS is one of my favorite people in the world. Of course, he lives in California and I rarely see him these days. That's probably why I still like him. We met in the early '70s in L.A. at the songwriter Jimmy Webb's birthday party. We were both so high we needed the Wichita Lineman to help us scratch our asses.

Indeed, the entire creative culture of the era seemed destined to drive in the fast lane. This death-bound determination sometimes led to truth and beauty and sometimes to death itself in a place called California that I have always regarded as a tow-away zone. Van Dyke's main curse, however, has been that everyone in Hollywood has always regarded him as a genius, and I am just smart enough to realize that for once they are right.

Soon after we met, Van Dyke and I formed a highly exclusive club called the Undepressibles. For the rest of our lives we agreed that nothing would ever depress us. If our best friend snapped his wig and wiped out his entire family, that didn't bother us. Death, life, suicide, divorce, drug overdoses, financial disasters, politics, parking tickets, or anything that could happen to anybody including ourselves meant nothing to the Undepressibles. And it worked for a while. Van Dyke and I recently agreed that the only thing that has depressed us at all is the passage of time. And time, of course, is the money of love.

Van Dyke has accomplished so much music and cultural history in his life it would seem like a fantasy to most of us. As a child actor, he played the recurring role of Little Tommy Manicotti on Jackie Gleason's *The Honeymooners*. He played keyboards on a number of albums by the Grateful Dead. He produced the first records of Randy Newman and Ry Cooder, and in 1971 he pioneered the first in the industry music videos for record promotion at Warner Bros.

Van Dyke also did the arrangements for the cello on the Beach Boys megahit "Good Vibrations," as well as collaborating with Brian Wilson on the visionary albums *Smile* and *Orange Crate Art*. And once, long ago, he was reading an anthropology magazine while "lettin' the possum out" and discovered that Australian aboriginals, on very cold nights, slept with three dogs.

"Goodness gracious, great balls of fire."

Out of this dreamtime dumper experience, Van Dyke Parks came up with the perfect name for the perfect, preeminent, pop-rock band of the seventies, Three Dog Night. To be fair, there are some who insist that Van Dyke did not name the group. To these voices in the wilderness Van Dyke responds, "I'm correct on naming Three Dog Night. It was me. No doubt about it. Everyone else was inhaling. It's a good thing the name was Three Dog Night because the record company wanted to call the band 'Tricycle.'"

Speaking of dogs, it wasn't just Brian Wilson singing on Van Dyke's *Orange Crate Art* album. The last track also features Parks's Scotty, Clementine. The dog with Van Dyke at the piano, however, is the four-year-old wirehaired fox terrier, Jubal, named after the first musician in the Bible. According to Van Dyke's wife, Sally, Jubal's full name is Cornpone Jubilation Early Christmas Gift Parks. A portion of his name, I am given to understand, derives from the Confederate General Jubal Early, who, like Jubal the dog, was so fast he often outran his supplies. That was part of the reason, according to Van Dyke, that he *almost* took Washington.

As well as being a member in full standing, no pun intended, of my band, the Texas Jewboys, Van Dyke and I once wrote a song together. (It was a little thing I had out a few years ago, until they made me put it back in.) The song is called "The Take-It-Easy Trailer Park." It has not been a financial pleasure for either of us, but what do we care? We're the Undepressibles.

P.S. Here are just a few of the artists for whom Van Dyke Parks has created musical arrangements: Aaron Neville, Meryl Streep, the Everly Brothers, U2, Three Dog Night, the Beach Boys, Natalie Cole, Carly Simon, Bonnie Raitt, Linda Ronstadt, Jennifer Warnes, Leo Kottke, Judy Collins, Bruce Springsteen, Phil Ochs, Ry Cooder, Cher, Arlo Guthrie, Sam Phillips, Lowell George and Little Feat, Ringo Starr, Keith Moon, Kinky Friedman, Harry Nilsson, Sheryl Crow, Randy Newman, T-Bone Burnett, and the Buena Vista Social Club.

Not bad for a kid who started out on *The Honeymooners*.

"You call this horseback riding?"

HANK WILLIAMS *and* HI-LIFE

HANK WILLIAMS'S SISTER, Irene, gave this photo to my friend Marty Stuart, and Marty sent it to me. It depicts country music's troublemaking genius in a rare moment of peace, riding his beloved Tennessee walking horse, Hi-Life. Marty says he loves this picture "because it cuts through the myth and shows what a down-to-earth country man Hank Williams really was."

More than any singer before or after, Hank's life, his death, and his music not only define what country is all about, but they make him the tragic, magic messenger sent here to heal a broken heart. For Hank, I believe, instinctively understood one of the greatest paradoxes of human existence: The only heart that is whole is one that has been broken.

Hank Williams died on January 1, 1953, on the road somewhere between Montgomery, Alabama, and Oak Hill,

West Virginia, a twenty-nine-year-old American prophet, a hillbilly Shakespeare, burning out of control like a country music comet exploding in the soul of every kid who ever wanted to be a country star.

Hank, like all of us, I suppose, was on his way to the show he never played. It was a New Year's Day gig in Canton, Ohio. My friend Bob Neuwirth was there as a young teenager and vividly remembers the stunning announcement of Hank's death to the crowd, and Red Foley and his band, from behind the drawn curtain, playing "Peace in the Valley."

It could simply be, as I've often maintained, that some people will do anything to get out of a gig in Canton, Ohio. That was just a joke, folks. Like life itself. The first commandment of country music, I believe, is Never Take Hank Williams More Seriously Than He Took Himself.

Several years ago, my pal in Hawaii, Will Hoover, introduced me to the late great Jerry Byrd, obviously before he became the late great Jerry Byrd, and he gave me some interesting insights into Hank. For those who haven't had their country music hip card punched, Jerry Byrd was the virtuoso steel-guitar player who in large part gave Hank his distinctive sound on many of his biggest hits. Jerry Byrd, indeed, was a musical tutor to Hank and the Drifting Cowboys both in the studio and on the road.

Jerry Byrd believed, from experience with Hank over his

brief, turbulent career, that if all country stars behaved like Hank, the fans would revolt. Hank's demons, according to Byrd, had driven him to the point at which he had very little regard for the fans, the band, and ultimately, of course, himself. No time for autographs was putting it mildly, as Jerry Byrd saw it. The irony was that in spite of his life spinning completely out of control and destroying him after four short years of stardom, his star has shined brightly ever since, reaching the hearts of millions of people around the globe.

My theory is that Hank had a little bit of Jesus and Mozart and van Gogh in him, and people are just plain perverse; they like you better when you're dead. That is, everybody

"Guess who's coming to dinner?"

except Bill Monroe, who had the unique gift of bringing flowers to the living. On one snowy December night when Hank came through Nashville for the last time, the folks at the Grand Ol' Opry didn't want him to come up and they certainly didn't want to go down and see him. He was only the biggest star they ever had. But it must be admitted, he was also a mess. Of the entire Opry cast, only Bill Monroe went down to the street, got in the Cadillac with Hank, and spoke to him in words that would be Nashville's final farewell to country music's greatest star.

May peace be with Hank and Hi-Life. May they be safe and sheltered from sorrow. May they ride like the wind. May they walk in peace. May they travel together the trails of their dreams.

DONNY OSMOND and SPIKE

I WAS AT THE Flamingo in Vegas recently playing the slots with my old pal Kent Perkins and his wife, the great Ruth Buzzi. Total strangers kept coming up to hug Ruth Buzzi and tell her how much they loved her. This was beginning to irritate me, not because I was jealous but because I was losing fairly disastrously with five dollars' worth of heroin on the spoon, and I didn't think this was helping my luck.

"Watching Kinky gamble is like watching a trainwreck," said Kent.

"Let's go see Donny and Marie," said Ruthie.

"In the words of Frank Sinatra," I said, "'I'm losing.'"

So we went to see Donny and Marie at the Flamingo, which was packed tighter than a can of smoked oysters. Because Ruthie had been a regular on the '70s television hit *Donny & Marie*, they gave us the best table in the house. I ordered an adult portion of Mexican mouthwash—tequila to you—and settled in to watch the show. Never having been a fan of Donny and Marie, I expected to go into a diabetic coma. This did not happen; it was one of the best shows I'd ever seen in my life.

It did get off to a bit of an abrupt start, however. I'd apparently nodded off in the first five minutes, and when I opened my eyes, Donny's smiling head was about one foot away from my own and the entire place was going crazy. Donny had come down to our table, evidently to welcome Ruth Buzzi personally. After that, I stayed awake, and I'm glad that I did.

Marie was terrific, of course. She's had eight kids and she looks like she's about twenty-four with talent written all over her. And then there's Donny. I wouldn't have said it in quite the same way, but I have to agree with my old pal Liz Smith: "I am here to tell you he is charmingly campy, good-looking and grand. . . . Donny is divine."

I wasn't prepared for Donny Osmond being funny as hell, poignant, powerful, and so seductively self-effacing you find yourself pulling for the guy, which is what being a star is all about. After all, here he is bickering with Marie, singing like a bird, doing strenuous, acrobatic, frenetic dance numbers, wowing the crowd, and—he's a grandfather. Amazing.

I wasn't one when I walked in, but I left the place a Donny and Marie fan. And it took me only fifty years. As things turned out, I didn't get very far. The Osmonds, apparently,

"I hate Marie."

had arranged for Ruthie, Kent, and myself to come backstage and hang out with them for a while. It hadn't been announced yet but Donny and Marie's contract with the Flamingo had just been extended through October 2010. I could understand why.

Donny may be one of the very few people whose lives have disproved F. Scott Fitzgerald's dictum that "there are no second acts in American lives." He is so pleasant and engaging to talk to, you almost forget that he is a member of that small fraternity of aristocratic freaks called teen idols for whom the future is supposed to be virtually nonexistent.

On December 10, 1963, one day after his sixth birthday, Donny made his debut on *The Andy Williams Show* singing "You Are My Sunshine." During the early to mid-seventies, "We lived our own version of 'A Hard Day's Night,'" he says. They also sold more records than anyone could have imagined. But throughout his twenties and into his thirties, "Not only could I not get arrested," he says, "but I was downright radioactive. But the best thing that happened to me was losing my career, my fame, my money, all gone. I could have gone to some Holiday Inn lounge and sung "Puppy Love" for the next twenty years."

Donny Osmond's success and reinvention have come not just by persistence and endurance but also with the realization that, in his words, "People grew up with me and I with them, and we all grew up with the same songs. That music was great for what it was, people loved it, it was incredibly successful. So I refused to be a prisoner of my teenybopper past."

Donny is a big animal lover and always had pets when he was growing up. "The pet is the perfect workout partner," he says. "He'll never stand you up." Currently, Donny has two birds who may or may not work the treadmill with him. Donny's dog, who always used to sleep on his shoulder, is Spike.

P.S. If you doubt my skills as a theater critic, take a tip from the Kinkster. Next time you're in Vegas, go to the Flamingo and see Donny and Marie. You'll be very glad you did.

"We trip the light fantastic on the sidewalks of New York."

F. MURRAY ABRAHAM *and* WOLFIE

I FIRST MET F. Murray Abraham and his wife, Kate, aboard the *QE2* on a trip from England to the United States, roughly retracing the route of the *Titanic*. For us, fortunately, the trip was uneventful. Perhaps "uneventful" is a poor choice of words—it's precisely the word Captain Edward John Smith of the *Titanic* used to describe his career at sea.

Murray and I were guest lecturers aboard the ship. Murray, or F, as I sometimes call him, was regaling the crowd with tales of his dazzlingly diverse acting career. I forgot what I was regaling the passengers about, but to a captive audience, even a stultifyingly dull existence can sometimes seem almost titillating. At least they didn't put either one of us in the brig.

Murray has starred in classical theater for much of his career, performing in many Shakespearean productions such as *Othello* and *Richard III*, as well as appearing in numerous plays ranging from Samuel Beckett to Gilbert and Sullivan, always my father's favorites. I'm convinced that part of his training for all this came about in his teenage years when he lived in El Paso and was a gang member along the Mexican border.

It is almost unbelievable that one person could possess the necessary range of talent to do everything that Murray has done. He appeared in *Serpico* (1973) and *All The President's Men* (1976), and moved seamlessly from a role as a talking leaf in Fruit of the Loom television commercials—at least it was a speaking part—to winning the Academy Award for Best Actor for his role as Antonio Salieri in *Amadeus* (1984).

Asked about the so-called Oscar jinx, he responded, "The Oscar is the single most important event of my career. I have dined with kings, shared equal billing with my idols, lectured at Harvard and Columbia. If this is a jinx, I'll take two."

What most of his fellow passengers, including myself, were totally unaware of was that in the same time frame Murray was filming *Amadeus* in Europe, he was also jetting back and forth to Florida to star as Omar Suarez, the drug dealer in *Scarface* with Al Pacino. The fact that F. Murray Abraham gave stellar performances in both roles at roughly the same time was amazing to me and my fellow passengers. As a wise guy in the audience observed, "You'd have to be bipolar just to get into character."

When asked what roles he would like to play in the future, Murray thought about it for a moment and then gave what I thought was a very interesting answer. "If I could do only *Star Trek* movies for the rest of my career," he said, "I would. That's how strongly I feel about this organization. I do not say that lightly."

As far as animals are concerned, Murray has narrated the PBS series *Nature*, about the animal kingdom, including "Dogs That Changed the World." Regarding his own pets, Murray wrote me the following: "My dog's name was Wolfie, short for Wolfgang; he was a standard poodle. Of all the dogs we've had, from cairns to bassets, to many mutts, Wolfie was THE BEST. I'll never have another breed. Everyone who knew Wolfie responded the same way when they saw him: They would smile. He died on Christmas Eve. I had no idea how much he meant to me until he was gone; for a year I couldn't think of him without tearing up. After all these years, as I think of Wolfie now, I smile. What a great dog."

"A little harder, and a little to the right."

LARRY DIERKER and BABE

LARRY DIERKER WAS drafted by the Houston Colt .45s/Astros at the ripe old age of seventeen. He made his major league pitching debut on September 22, 1964, his eighteenth birthday, and struck out Willie Mays in the first inning. As of this writing, he remains the last man to play in the majors at such a young age.

"As I look back," said Dierker, "I think I was born to play baseball. I was always one of the tallest kids and could throw harder than any of them right up through high school. After I signed with the Colt .45s, the general manager, Paul Richards, came to see some of us in the rookie league. He taught me to throw a slider in about five minutes. It was so easy; I couldn't believe I hadn't come up with it on my own. That one pitch, along with good velocity and enough control to throw strikes, allowed me to leap from high school to the major leagues in a single bound. The manager said I was able to make the grade so young because I had ice water in my veins."

To accomplish what Larry Dierker did, going right from high school seamlessly and successfully into the major leagues, would be a virtual impossibility today. In fact, it's a rarity even for truly gifted college players to segue straight into the major leagues with any degree of success or longevity. Dierker, however, managed to survive and thrive in the majors, pitching for fourteen years, from 1964 to 1977, first with the Colt 45s/Astros and then with the St. Louis Cardinals, both of the National League. He was not only the youngest pitcher ever to strike out Willie Mays, he was also one of the very few pitchers ever to hit a home run off Nolan Ryan.

From 1997 to 2001, Dierker managed the Houston Astros. Houston finished in first place in four of those five years. In 1998 he was elected National League Manager of the Year. He has written two books, *It Ain't Brain Surgery* and *My Team*, in which he reflects upon the greatest players he's been witness to in his years of baseball.

I first met Larry and his wife, Judy, at a Bonefit concert in Houston raising funding for Utopia Animal Rescue Ranch. Later, they drove up to the ranch to visit with Cousin Nancy, Tony, and myself. At lunch in Kerrville it was evident that Larry Dierker has a lot of fans, and I must report he was very gracious with them. Of course, I'm very gracious with my fans, as well. Unfortunately, most of mine are attached to the ceiling.

"Babe," says Larry, "is not much of a retriever. She won't fetch anything, only swims to cool off, and isn't much of a watchdog either because she loves all people and hates all dogs. I think she's a lapdog trapped in a Lab body."

"She curls up with Stanley the cat," said Judy.

"Babe sounds pretty smart to me," I said. "She's also got a great name for a ballplayer's dog."

"Judy is the true animal lover in the family," said Larry.

"Larry is a natural at baseball," said Judy, "but he's not quite a natural yet with animals. But the animals are teaching him."

"Have you ever thought about adding a little color to your wardrobe?"

MARK TWAIN *and* BAMBINO, AMONG OTHERS

SAMUEL CLEMENS, A sickly child not expected to live, did not become a political leader or a man of great wealth or power. He may not have become the greatest man in the world. That curse, inexorably, would fall upon Abraham Lincoln. Yet Clemens accomplished something that may well have given him an equal claim to lasting significance. He created Mark Twain. And Mark Twain, of course, defined the age.

Licensed as a riverboat pilot in 1858, Clemens took the name "Mark Twain" from the navigational term meaning two fathoms, or twelve feet deep, safe to go forward. Armed with only a righteous sense of humor, a cigar, and the stories of his childhood, that is exactly what he did. Along with Huckleberry Finn and the slave Jim, he sailed into history.

In 1885, the people weren't as civilized as we are today; they were blissfully ignorant of the term "N-word." Accordingly, the argot of the gutter was the language of the day, as, of course, it still is. Mark Twain, therefore, perhaps wishing to accurately convey the human condition, used the word "nigger" more than two hundred times in *Huckleberry Finn*. Nevertheless, many in the literary community have hailed this work as the greatest novel written in the Western world (some favor *Moby-Dick*, Melville's compelling masterpiece which, for more than five decades could be found only in the whaling sections of bookstores).

Professor Jocelyn Chadwick, the highly respected African American scholar, has spent much of her time over the years defending Mark Twain and *Huckleberry Finn* from those who wish to decry the author as a racist and ban his greatest work. Professor Chadwick finds that the attacks come about equally from the left as well as the right. She speaks before library associations, school boards, city councils, etc., to remind them that Mark Twain has made an incalculable, enduring contribution to our culture by creating *Huckleberry Finn* and interweaving the character of the runaway slave, Jim, into white society. "Jim," she says, "is a man of decency, integrity, and humanity, in a world full of scoundrels and hypocrites."

Animals can be scoundrels, too, but you'll never catch them being hypocrites. Whatever he thought of people in general, Mark Twain loved animals, especially cats. Growing up in Hannibal, Missouri, his family is said to have shared their home with as many as nineteen cats at the same time. Mark Twain always had pet cats living with him, and he included cats in many of his stories. "I simply can't resist a cat, particularly a purring one," he said. "They are the cleanest, cunningest, and most intelligent things I know, outside of the girl you love, of course."

Twain continues on the theme: "By what right has the dog come to be regarded as a 'noble' animal? The more brutal and cruel and unjust you are to him, the more your fawning and adoring slave he becomes; whereas, if you shamefully misuse a cat once she will always maintain a dignified reserve toward you afterward—you will never get her full confidence again."

Several years ago I had the honor of giving a lecture and a reading at the Pen Warmed-up in Hell writers' series at the Mark Twain Library in Hartford, Connecticut. In the library there is a testimonial written by one of Mark Twain's servants, Kate Leary, which captures a bit of the spirit of the man and the times. It reads as follows:

Mr. Clemens borrowed a kitten one time, called Bambino, from Clara, who had him in the sanitarium, and had trained him to wash his own face in the bowl every morning—which shows that he was a very smart little cat.

He used to have this kitten up in his room at the Fifth Avenue house and he taught it to put out a light, too. He had a tiny little lamp to light his cigars with at the head of his bed, and after he got all fixed and didn't want the light anymore, he taught that cat to put his paw on the light and put it out. Bambino would jump on the bed, look at Mr. Clemens to see if he was through with the light, and when Mr. Clemens would bow twice to him, he'd jump over to the table quick, and put his little paw right on the lamp! Mr. Clemens was always showing him off, he did that for a lot of people that came there to call.

One night he [Bambino, not Clemens] got kind of gay, when he heard some cats calling from the back fence, so he found a window open and he stole out. We looked high and low but we couldn't find him. Mr. Clemens felt so bad that he advertised in all the papers for him. He offered a reward for anybody that would bring the cat back. My goodness! The people that came bringing cats to that house! A perfect stream! They all wanted to see Mr. Clemens, of course.

Two or three nights after, Katherine heard a cat meowing across the street in General Sickles' back yard, and there was Bambino—large as life! So she brought him right home. Mr. Clemens was delighted and then he advertised that his cat was found. But the people kept coming just the same with all kinds of cats for him—anything to get a glimpse of Mr. Clemens!

When I'd finished my reading and questions and answers with the crowd at the Mark Twain Library, they graciously gave me a guided after-hours tour of the Mark Twain House. Like all the people bringing their cats, I'd been hoping to get a glimpse of Mr. Clemens. Perhaps I did. There was one of his cigars in an ashtray in the upstairs billiard room that he loved. (Because of an incident some years back when Garrison Keillor hit a cue ball with a stick, practically dissolving it into dust, no one is allowed to play pool on the table. They did, however, allow me to briefly—and reverently, I might add—fondle Twain's balls.)

But it was clear from the outset that Mark Twain and all the cats he loved had left the building. The cigar had been dead for nearly a hundred years—so, too, Mark Twain and all of his friends, foes, children, critics, and cats. Only Tom Sawyer and Becky Thatcher lived happily ever after. Only Huck Finn and Jim will live forever.

As Mark Twain himself once wrote, "I've had many problems in my life, most of which never happened."

"Help! I'm getting carpal shoulder syndrome."

MOLLY IVINS *and* KAYE NORTHCAT

PUT QUITE SIMPLY, Molly Ivins was the conscience of Texas politics. Even in death, she remains living proof that you can be firmly on the left, speak the truth, and still be funny as hell. At the time of her death, on January 31, 2007, her books were all bestsellers, she was syndicated in more than four hundred newspapers, and her voice remained as strong as it does today, a Texas Cassandra, if you will, warning the world that we have to do better or we will all suffer the consequences of our spiritual and political complacency.

Of the cancer that killed her, she had this to say: "First, they mutilate you, then they poison you, then they burn you. I have been on blind dates better than that."

Regarding the first President Bush's efforts to play the Texan, she wrote, "Real Texans do not use 'summer' as a verb." Regarding his son, "If you think his daddy had trouble with 'the vision thing,' wait'll you meet this one." She is also credited with having coined the nickname "Shrub" for George W. Bush. Indeed, Molly once described him thusly: "There was the president at his press conference looking just like a turtle on a fence post."

Molly Ivins was a big, brazen cowgirl who once walked into a party and said, "That boy's jeans are on so tight, if he farted he'd blow his boots off." After Pat Buchanan's speech at the 1992 Republican convention, she wrote, "It was good, but I liked it better in the original German." And Molly once described Dallas as "the town that roots for Goliath to beat David."

Though she was, unquestionably, the sparkling and irreverent voice of the American left, and a three-time Pulitzer Prize finalist, she always claimed that her two greatest honors were that the Minneapolis police force named its mascot pig after her, and that she was once banned from the campus of Texas A & M.

In 1976 she began writing for the *New York Times*, whose lifeless, staid, not to say stultifyingly dull style proved too much for the unsinkable Molly after six years of "being miserable for five times the salary." Her colorful prose continually clashed with her constipated, humorless editors' expectations, so in 1982 they let her go after she wrote about a "community chicken-killing festival," describing it as a "gang-pluck."

My dad, Tom, was a hero in World War II and Molly had long been one of his heroes, though he'd never met her. After Tom had a heart attack, Molly simply appeared at our doorstep in Austin one afternoon just to visit with him. Molly lifted Tom's spirits tremendously, and her gesture touched him deeply, as it did his son.

When I announced my intention to run for governor of Texas in 2005, Molly asked me why I wanted to be governor. I answered, "Why the hell not?" Molly said, "That's perfect, that's beautiful. That's your campaign slogan." And, indeed, it was. Ever since then, if there's something I want to do in life but I'm not quite sure if I should, I remember Molly's suggestion and I ask myself, "Why the hell not?"

Being the conscience of Texas was, as you might suspect, a full-time job, yet Molly still found time throughout her life to love and consort with animals not of the two-legged variety. The Siamese cat seen draped over her left shoulder as she writes is named Kaye Northcat, after her longtime coeditor at the *Texas Observer*, Kaye Northcott. Molly also had two beloved black standard poodles named Athena and Fanny Brice.

The most unusual pet Molly ever had, however, was probably the large black dog that wandered into her life while she was working for the *Observer*. The dog had an uncanny skill for getting underfoot and in the way of people, causing them to stumble or trip and invariably shout, "Shit!" which, of course, became the name of the dog. It was a humorous experience just to watch this large, brash

Texas woman calling the dog loudly by name. Molly always claimed she'd been waiting all her life for the perfect excuse to be able to repeatedly yell "Shit!" in public.

But I'll let Molly tell you in her own words.

WHAT'S IN A NAME?
by Molly Ivins

Shit the Dog finally croaked on December 9 after fourteen and a half years of marplotting through life. Shit was the *Texas Observer*'s office dog in the early 1970s and, as such, did a lot to hold down the circulation of the magazine. Many who knew Shit consider her possibly the most worthless dog that ever lived, but they overlook her great talent—Shit had a genius for fouling things up.

As *Observer* dog, it was her invariable habit to greet all our readers who had faithfully climbed up three flights of stairs in order to renew their subscriptions, by growling and snapping at them. Whereas, whenever some nut arrived at the office to scream about the communist propaganda we were publishing, she would frisk right up with her tail wagging to kiss him enthusiastically. She was also wont to contribute to the ambiance by going downstairs to pee on the landlord's rug. Our landlord was Judge Sam Houston Clinton, now on the court of Criminal Appeals: he tended to be a little humorless about those episodes.

Her politics weren't all bad: she once bit hell out of Col. Wilson Speir, head of the Texas Rangers. Shit never met another dog she didn't like and on the whole she liked people indiscriminately as well. She did have, however, strong prejudices against bicycle riders, uniformed law-enforcement personnel, and pregnant women. She spent much of her waking life getting into the neighbors' garbage and was fond of strewing it about generously. The acquisition of food was her major life interest and for this purpose she developed a fabulous impersonation of a starving dog. The fact that she was grossly fat much of her life only made the impersonation more impressive. Shit also liked to sleep a lot and never failed to sack out where she would cause maximum inconvenience, at the exact center of the traffic pattern, so people would either have to step over her or trip over her.

I never intended to name the dog Shit. Kaye Northcott foisted the little black puppy on me with a heartless ploy— left her with me "just for the weekend" and then returned Monday threatening to take her to the pound and have her put to sleep. I was going to name her something lovely, like Athena, but reality intervened. She was the only dog I ever saw that could trip on the pattern in the linoleum, so we called her Shitface for a while, and then it got to be Shit for short and then it was too late.

In her younger years, Shit loved nothing so much as going on camping trips, where the opportunities for getting into trouble were almost limitless. Any trip on which she did not manage to fall into the cactus, steal the steaks, and turn over a few canoes, she considered a waste of time. I developed nerves of tungsten.

When I took Shit to New York in 1976, many people told me it was cruel to keep a ranch-raised dog in a big city. Of course she adored New York—so much garbage to get into, so many dogs to meet, so little exercise. In a city full of Tsing Luck-poos and Shar-peis, people would look at Shit and say, "Oh, what breed is that one?"

"Purebred Texas blackhound," I always said, and they would nod knowingly and say they'd heard those Texas blackhounds were splendid dogs.

Shit once caused gridlock on the entire Upper West Side. I had found a parking space right in front of my building and so let Shit out of the car off her leash, as it was only a few steps to the door. Most unfortunately, a bicycle rider passed at that very moment. Shit charged into the street barking and snapping at the man, who had a baby in a small seat on the back of the bike. I tried not to call the dog in public, but I could see her knocking over the bike and the baby getting hurt. Clearly an emergency, so I let loose, "SHIT! SHIT!" This caused several neighborhood children to appear out of nowhere and to begin chanting in chorus while pointing at me, "She said a dirty word, she said a dirty word." The guy on the bike, justifiably upset about having been attacked by this beast, got off in the middle of the street and wheeled around yelling, "I'll have the law on you, lady. Letting your dog run loose without a leash is illegal in this city. That animal is a menace. I'm calling the cops."

In the meantime, a woman with an unrelated grievance over the parking space I had just occupied came marching down the block, arms akimbo, saying, "You have some nerve, you went right ahead and took that parking place, you saw us waiting there, but you went right ahead and took it, I can't believe your nerve, we were there first but you took that place. . . ." The kids kept chanting, the biker kept screaming, the lady kept bitching, Shit started running around everybody in circles, traffic came to a halt, then backed up through the red light, then two red lights, people got out of their cars to see what was going on, other people farther back started honking, Shit was delirious with the excitement of it all, the cops came, she attacked the cops, by this time traffic was backed up all the way up Amsterdam and down Columbus. A typical Shit performance.

I loved Shit, but she was quite wearing. I used to think wistfully that other dogs got dognapped or hit by cars. . . . Then one day, Shit did get hit by a car but she didn't die: it just cost me $700 to get her leg fixed. She gimped around thereafter on this bionic leg, becoming more Shit-like by the year. The dog was a catalyst for trouble, disruption, uproar, consternation, confusion, and bedlam.

She went out with the style we had come to expect from her—hit by a car, but no mere dead dog by the side of the road. Nope, biggest mess you ever saw and it had to be cleared up by Northcott and myself. We got most of her remains into Kaye's plastic laundry basket and took her down to the pound, the two of us a pair of poorly matched pallbearers. The people at the pound were kind, but said they had to fill out a form. They needed my name. My address. And I waited one last time for the question I had answered a thousand times from bemused strangers, enraged neighbors, at kennels, veterinarians' offices, dog pounds, and police stations. "What is the dog's name?"

I had Shit for almost fifteen years. It seemed longer.

First published in the Texas Observer, *February 1987*

RUTH BUZZI and GLADYS

Everybody loves Ruth Buzzi. If you don't, you're liable to get whacked on the head with her purse. Ruthie, a true American icon, is also a dear friend of mine, and I say without prejudice, she's one of the funniest people alive.

Everyone who knows and loves Ruth Buzzi, and that's just about everyone, seems to have seen her work at different times and different places. Many who, like myself, are old enough to sleep alone, remember her from the huge and influential TV hit show *Rowan & Martin's Laugh-In*, which ran from 1968 to 1975. Ruthie was one of only four people to appear in every single episode, the other three being Rowan and Martin themselves and Gary Owens.

Before *Laugh-In*, Ruth starred in *The Entertainers*, appeared in the Broadway musical *Sweet Charity*, was a regular as Marlo Thomas's friend on *That Girl*, and appeared on *The Steve Allen Comedy Hour*. It was the character sketches on Steve Allen that led to her being cast for the new NBC show that would revolutionize television comedy, *Laugh-In*.

On *Laugh-In*, Ruth developed many memorable characters. Her versatility as a comedian was such that she could play everything from flashy hookers to Southern belles to Burbank Airlines stewardesses. Among her recurring characters were Busybody Buzzi, Hollywood gossip columnist; Doris Swizzler, cocktail lounge habitué who always got hilariously hammered with husband Leonard (Dick Martin); and her most famous character, the dowdy spinster Gladys Ormphby, clad in brown, with her bun inexorably covered by a visible hairnet. Her purse was a lethal weapon, and she would flail away at anyone seeking to take advantage of her. Arte Johnson's dirty old man character, Tyrone, was most often the culprit. Tyrone would accost Gladys and ask, "Do you believe in the hereafter?" Gladys snapped back, "Of course I do!" Tyrone shot back, "Then you know what I'm *here* after!"

Ruthie won a Golden Globe for her work on *Laugh-In*, became a regular part of Dean Martin's Celebrity Roasts, and then completed a highly successful seven-year hitch on *Sesame Street*. She has guest-starred on so many television series and specials it would be tedious to mention them all. It's enough to say she always leaves 'em laughing.

I met Ruthie many years ago through her husband, Kent Perkins, who's a rather humorous individual himself. Kent

"Don't tell her, I just ate her purse."

told me that Ruthie came from a long line of Italian barbers and would be happy to cut my hair, which needed cutting because when I took off my cowboy hat it looked like a Lyle Lovett Starter Kit. Anyway, my hair was very thick and very kinky and Ruthie graciously cut and shaped it better than any haircut I'd ever had. So, over the years, I kept coming back to Ruthie for haircuts.

Many years later Ruthie told me the secret of how she could cut my hair so well. Her father had not been a barber; he'd been a sculptor and monument builder. Ruthie had gotten all her experience for cutting my hair from trimming the hedges of a graveyard.

Ruth Buzzi loves animals, currently sponsors a pen at Utopia Rescue Ranch, and has done a number of free appearances to raise funding for us. She has about ninety-seven different kinds of animals on the farm where she and Kent live, including a cat named Ratso, who flies first class so much he knows the flight attendants, and a horse named Gladys. Every time Ruth pulls up to the farm in her pickup truck and rolls down the window, Gladys sticks her head inside the truck and Ruth gives her horse a favorite treat, a Mrs. Baird's Fried Apple Pie.

Ruthie, along with Richard Moll of *Night Court*, once did a hilarious performance on a video for my song "Get Your Biscuits in the Oven (And Your Buns in the Bed)." During the course of that video, she hit me repeatedly over the head with her purse. By the time she was through, it had flattened my cowboy hat so it looked like I was wearing a black tortilla.

But I wasn't mad. I'd just been initiated into a very select and time-honored fraternity. Here, in a random and haphazard order, are some of the other people Ruth Buzzi has clobbered with her purse: Bob Hope, Dean Martin, Frank Sinatra, John Wayne, John Lennon, and Muhammad Ali.

And you know what? We probably all deserved it.

"How many cats did it take to make that jacket?"

PHYLLIS DILLER *and* MISS KITTY

IMPORTANT CORRESPONDENCE FROM the desks of Miss Kitty and Ms. Diller: Miss Kitty is a Maine coon cat. She and Ms. Diller live in a large English-style home in Brentwood Park, Los Angeles. "The place used to be haunted," says Ms. Diller, "but the ghosts haven't been back since the night I tried on all my wigs." Miss Kitty is in business. She catches lizards and mice.

Ms. Diller is also in business. It started in 1955 when she was a thirty-seven-year-old working housewife with five kids who wanted to do stand-up comedy. Her husband, Sherwood Diller, encouraged her to prepare a nightclub act, which she soon did and got herself booked into San Francisco's Purple Onion. On March 7, 1955, the club booked her for a two-week run. She stayed for eighty-nine weeks. Within five years she'd made it to Carnegie Hall.

Phyllis Diller has starred in three television series and

has made guest appearances on hundreds of hit TV shows and countless specials, including twenty-two with her "idol," Bob Hope. When Hope took her with him on his Vietnam Christmas Tour, he told reporters, "If Phyllis had cooked for the enemy, the war would've been over in three days."

"I love TV," she says. "It's not my fault if the tubes blow out when I laugh." She has appeared in scores of movies, acted on stage (a highlight was her portrayal of Dolly Gallagher Levi in the Broadway production of *Hello, Dolly!*), and written four bestselling books. Yet it's her live performances that probably best capture the essence of Phyllis Diller.

She writes most of her own material, strictly avoiding off-color jokes. She kills audiences with jokes about her figure or lack thereof, the efforts made by medical science to make her more attractive, her mother-in-law, her face-lifts, her next-door neighbor. There seems to be no method or logic to her material, but she meticulously edits her words. She is said to be capable of delivering as many as twelve punch lines per minute. That is about as rapid-fire as Henny Youngman on marching powder. And one more thing— she's almost always funny. I've always wondered how she does it. She doesn't even seem to be miserable.

When she's not busy being funny, there is another side of Phyllis Diller that many of her fans are unaware of. It's kind of a Paul Harvey The Rest of the Story situation. Phyllis always wanted to be a concert pianist, going so far as to study at the Sherwood Conservatory in Chicago. But marriage and work and her "other career" seemed to make that dream an impossible one. Not so. From 1972 to 1982, she somehow managed to find the time to perform with more than a hundred symphony orchestras as piano soloist, her forte being Beethoven and Bach.

"I may look like a lampshade in a whorehouse when I go on stage," she says, but my sources say she has one of the largest, most elegant wardrobes in the world. Good for her, though there are many who no doubt miss the lampshade in the whorehouse. That being as it may, Ms. Diller continues to do some film roles in what has to be one of the most successful and enduring show business careers of all time. And not to be outdone, Miss Kitty is still catching lots of lizards and mice.

"I'm ready for my close-up now."

BUD CORT and LILLIAN

FIRST I WAS a fan of Bud Cort's; then I became a friend. He is, of course, a brilliant actor, writer, and director, but it does seem amazing that one person in one lifetime could accomplish so much, become close friends with so many fascinating people, make it look easy to be true to his craft, be an avid animal lover, be nominated for something every time he turns around, be funny as hell, and still be younger than me.

I first saw Bud in *Mash* and *Brewster McCloud* and, of course, the role that really got everybody's attention in the world, his stellar performance in the American classic *Harold and Maude*.

"*Harold and Maude* was one of the three best scripts I'd ever read," says Bud. "It was just an exercise in perfection. Including the occasional happy accident. Harold gets out of the car, the wind blows his trench coat open, you see a bit of red. He goes to the other side of the car, and a rainbow appears in the sky. You can't order a rainbow."

For Bud's work in *Harold and Maude* he was awarded the Crystal Star for Best Actor from the Academy of Cinema in Paris, as well as receiving a Golden Globe nomination for Best Actor for the film. Bud, at the time, was the youngest actor ever to be given an Homage by the Cinémathèque Française, joining the ranks of Charlie Chaplin, Sir Laurence Olivier, Orson Welles, and Buster Keaton.

Bud was a close friend not only of Orson Welles, but off and on for about seven years he lived in Groucho Marx's mansion until Marx's death in 1977. "He was my idol," says Bud. "I was his chorus boy. He had me singing for everyone from Mae West to Bob Dylan."

Bud Cort had three great-grandfathers, all fishermen, all lost at sea. Also, while recording an album in Paris, he stayed at L'Hôtel, where Oscar Wilde had lived—in the very room in which Oscar had died, famously remarking just before his death, "Either me or this wallpaper has got to go." Bud won't say what he thought of the wallpaper.

In the 1980s Bud had a Boston terrier named Lillian. He took her on a plane once by smuggling her on in a large carry-on camera bag. His plane was late getting into Minnesota, and he and Lillian had to rush to the theater where he was to appear in a play.

He and Lillian were both exhausted when they arrived

at the theater, so he placed the case under an empty seat and dashed backstage through a side entrance. By this time, the play had already begun and a cast member was delivering a quietly spoken monologue that kept being interrupted by what seemed to Bud to be a familiar sound. It was Lillian snoring. Lillian, according to Bud, always snored very loudly.

So Bud, as surreptitiously as possible under the circumstances, dashed back to where he'd left Lillian, and, of course, she wasn't there. The theater floor was at an incline and the bag and Lillian had rolled forward somewhere closer to the stage. So now Bud, on hands and knees, was trying to make his way through the audience to attempt to find Lillian before the entire performance went into the toilet. When Bud at last found her and picked her up, the audience gave them both a standing ovation.

"Is that jambalaya on your leg,
or are you just happy to see me?"

DR. JOHN, LUCY, and MORDECAI

THE FIRST TIME I saw Dr. John perform was in 1973 in Chattanooga, Tennessee, and he blew me away like a music hurricane. My band, the Texas Jewboys, was co-billed with him and it was our first tour and we thought we were very hot and very colorful. That is, until we saw Dr. John the Night Tripper take the stage, and the audience, by storm.

It was like being a participant-observer of a traveling Mardi Gras, and the music and the costumes and the colors blended together and awe-struck you like a child. Adorned with voodoo charms and regalia, Dr. John mesmerized the crowd with a show that included two megahits he had out that year, "Right Place, Wrong Time" and "Such a Night."

One thing that impressed me very much about that performance was Dr. John's practice of tossing gold and silver glitter out over the audience, a practice I was later to borrow—okay, steal. I did it so much, in fact, that it began to irritate people. Country audiences in particular did not relate to this colorful affectation, not being as hip as Dr. John's crowd. Of course, nobody was as hip as Dr. John's crowd. Eventually, I had to stop tossing out the sparkling stuff of dreams altogether, but the damage had already been done. In Nashville, they were derisively calling me "the man who put the glitter on Loretta Lynn's titter." But Dr. John continues to let the good times roll.

Dr. John, or Mac Rebennack, as he's known to his intimates, is the living embodiment of that rich musical heritage and emotional history that are unique to New Orleans. In the fifties he wrote and played guitar on some of the greatest records to come out of the Crescent City, including work by Professor Longhair, Art Neville, Frankie Ford, and Joe Tex. Mac's career as a guitarist ended when his ring finger was injured by a gunshot while defending singer-keyboardist Ronnie Barron, a bandmate and old friend. Mac turned to bass and then to piano and organ.

In 1963 he moved to L.A., where he played on records with Van Morrison, Aretha Franklin, Canned Heat, and Sonny and Cher. In 1968, with the album *Gris-gris*, he combined voodoo mysticism, chants, funk, rhythm & blues, creole roots, and psychedelic rock. With *Gris-gris*, *Dr. John's Gumbo*, and the seminal New Orleans funk album *In the Right Place*, Mac became influential around the world not only as the preeminent interpreter of New Orleans funk, but also its most authentic and charismatic ambassador.

Dr. John has recorded with the Rolling Stones, Carly Simon, James Taylor, and Neil Diamond, as well as playing on and coproducing Van Morrison's *A Period of Transition* (1977). He's done vocals for Popeyes Chicken & Biscuits ("Luv dat chicken" jingle) as well as scoring the film version of John Steinbeck's *Cannery Row* and appearing in Martin Scorsese's *The Last Waltz*. I wasn't present for the Popeyes jingle but I was there at *The Last Waltz* (I think!) when Dr. John joined the Band in a brilliant rendition of "Such a Night."

"The music makes me feel good," says Mac, "and it's my job to make the people feel good." It's a job he does better than virtually anybody else.

And now I'm pleased to present Dr. John's wife, Cat, to tell us about their dog: "Lucy was rescued from the pound in 1993 and has evolved into an incredibly noble lady of a dog. She loved the water more than anything, but had the quirk of being a terrible swimmer (unheard of considering her genetic heritage of Lab and pointer), but people would laugh just watching her splash. She did get better over time.

"When I was an outreach worker in New York City distributing condoms to hookers and clean needles to addicts, we had some bright green menthol-flavored condoms that Lucy liked and apparently ate. I discovered this to my horror as I was walking her and people began to laugh and point to her rear end. The poor thing was constipated for a week.

"The 'door' is the only still-standing remnant of the original cabin on our property. I'd been asking Mac to pose with Lucy out there forever and finally I had to just drag him out there in the cold one morning in his pajamas. I'm glad I did. We lost our Lucy just a few weeks after this was taken.

"Mordecai [the pug pictured on page 142], sadly, ran under a car in Montauk many years ago. But he could sing, sounding a bit demonic. Nevertheless, he sang well enough to be recorded by Mac's engineer on numerous occasions."

"Such a night!"

FATS DOMINO *and*
WINNIE THE POOH

ANTOINE "FATS" DOMINO Jr., one of nine children, was born in New Orleans in 1928. The first language he learned to speak was French. He played piano and sang as a child, and first performed in public at the ripe old age of ten. Fats still lives in New Orleans with his wife, Rosemary, with whom he's had eight children.

Fats Domino's first recording session at Cosimo Matassa's J&M studios in New Orleans is now a matter of historical as well as musical significance. The date was December 10, 1949, and Fats had just signed with Imperial Records. He cut eight tracks, one of which, "The Fat Man," was adapted from an old street song called "Junker's Blues." The song, clearly about drugs, was cleaned up for his first commercial release, and, to the surprise of almost everybody, went to

"Yes, he always dresses like this."

#2 on the R & B charts and reportedly sold a million copies, though no one is exactly sure. What a great many musical historians are sure about today is that this was most likely the first rock-and-roll record ever made.

Three years later, in 1952, "Goin' Home" became the first of nine #1 hits for Fats on the R & B charts. Between 1952 and 1959, those nine hits topped the charts for a combined total of fifty-one weeks, giving him almost an entire year's worth of chart supremacy. Domino would go on to sell more records (sixty-five million) than any other rocker of the fifties except Elvis Presley. Perhaps more important, he is widely regarded as one of the single most significant links between rhythm & blues and rock and roll.

"Ain't That a Shame," in 1955, topped the R & B charts for eleven weeks and broke into the pop charts by midsummer, making it the first of thirty-seven crossover hits for him in the next eight years. "Blueberry Hill," in 1956, a song I remember fondly from what I'm pleased to call my youth, was Domino's biggest Top 40 hit ever, reaching #2 on the pop charts (Guy Mitchell's megahit "Singin' the Blues" kept it from reaching the #1 position). It's a little-known piece of spiritual trivia, but it's true: Neither Fats Domino nor Creedence Clearwater Revival ever had a #1 hit on the pop charts.

In 1968, Domino's last single to make *Billboard*'s Top 100 was his cover version of the Beatles' "Lady Madonna." Some say the song was "affectionately written" by Paul McCartney in the Domino style. Fats was inducted into the Rock and Roll Hall of Fame at its first induction dinner on January 23, 1986. The following year he received a Lifetime Achievement Award at the 29th annual Grammy Awards.

Fats Domino's beloved bichon frise, named Winnie the Pooh, perished in Hurricane Katrina. The entire area was inundated, and when searchers could not find Fats at home, it was thought that he himself had drowned in the floodwaters as well. But that was not the case. When they finally found him, he was looking for Winnie the Pooh.

MARTY STUART *and*
OSCAR LEE PERKINS

MARTY STUART MAY look like a young little booger, but the truth is he's always been a veteran soul. A virtuoso mandolin and guitar player as a child, he'd already turned pro by twelve and was performing regular gigs with the bluegrass group the Sullivans.

It was around this early stage that Marty met Roland White, who played with the country music icon Lester Flatt. This led to an invitation for Marty to play a Labor Day gig with Flatt in Delaware. The year was 1972 and Marty was all of thirteen years old, but apparently he kicked ass enough to really impress wise old Lester Flatt. Flatt, indeed, was so impressed that he invited Marty to join his band permanently and took responsibility for managing the young teenager's continued education. Marty stayed with the bluegrass master until Flatt retired in 1978 for health reasons. Lester Flatt would die the following year, but the musical education and the emotional and historical heritage Marty absorbed from touring with Flatt were unique and incalculable.

Marty moved on to picking with such greats as fiddle-player Vassar Clements and guitarist Doc Watson. Marty also was one of the youngest, if not the youngest, people in Nashville getting regular session work. Then, in 1980, he was invited to join Johnny Cash's band. Two years later Marty recorded his first solo album, *Busy Bee Café*, and the following year he married Cash's daughter Cindy.

Marty was supposed to have been a wild child when he was younger but, unfortunately, I didn't know him then. By the time I met him, it was not in a bar but in a bookstore when he very graciously dropped by one of my book signings in the Nashville area. His once infamous "flamboyantly hedonist" party image was a thing of the past, he assured me. He was now a born-again Christian and recorded both country and gospel records. "I won't hold that against you," I told him.

Having divorced Cindy Cash and also having won his freedom from several record labels, Marty married Grand Ole Opry star Connie Smith in 1997. There's a poignant story about how they met. It was back in the sixties when Marty was just a kid, albeit a very talented and precocious one. His folks took him to see a Connie Smith concert and

"Busted flat in Baton Rouge, waitin' for a train."

afterward, he told his mother that someday he would marry her. His mother, I'm sure, said, "Of course, son."

In 1998 he helped produce and wrote eight songs on Connie's comeback album on Warner Bros. Marty himself soon released a number of records in fairly rapid succession: *The Pilgrim, Country Music, Soul's Chapel, Badlands*, and the bluegrass *Live at the Ryman*, in 2006. Marty also was nominated for a Golden Globe for Best Original Score for the movie *All the Pretty Horses*.

Marty was generous enough to record my song "Lady Yesterday" on a tribute album to the Kinkster. I believe I'm the only living artist with two tribute albums. That, of course, depends how you define living.

From 1996 to 2002, Marty served as president of the Country Music Foundation, which oversees the Country Music Hall of Fame. He also has the most extensive collection of country music memorabilia in the world. You really ought to see it. It's like Nashville's attic.

Marty no longer wears fancy rhinestone-studded Nudie suits onstage. He now wears black in honor of the passing of his friend and former father-in-law, Johnny Cash. I also wear black, but I do it so I don't have to wash my clothes. If Marty and I ever show up at the same party, one of us is going to have to leave.

Oh, yeah. Marty also has a great new show on cable's RFD-TV. *The Marty Stuart Show* features traditional country music in the spirit of *The Porter Wagoner Show*, *Flatt & Scruggs*, and *Hee Haw*. It features music by Marty, his band, the Fabulous Superlatives, his wife Connie Smith, and special guests.

Here's what Marty says about his dog, Oscar Lee Perkins: "I named Oscar after Jerry Lee Lewis, Carl Perkins, and Oscar Sullivan from the country comedy duo Lonzo & Oscar. I might have a thousand other dogs in my lifetime, however, Oscar will always hold a special place in my heart. He was a showbiz hound dog. He loved to have his picture made. As a matter of fact, when we were leaving the set at the end of this photo shoot, Oscar remarked, 'Kinky Friedman will probably be calling to put us in his book.' I said, 'Do you think he'll pay?' Oscar replied, 'Oh, Kinky's a good guy. He'll throw us a bone.'"

"On your mark, get set, go."

PENN JILLETTE, SHIRLEY TEMPLE, TURTLE, ZOLTEN, MOXIE, TELLER, FONEBONE, and FENSTERBENSTER

SHERLOCK HOLMES ONCE said, "What you do in this world is a matter of no consequence. The question is, 'what can you make people believe that you have done?'" This brilliant commentary on the human condition is applicable to the equally brilliant Penn and Teller. Like Sherlock, they are not in the habit of revealing their methods. They have been my friends since Christ was a cowboy, however, and over the years, they may have revealed to me an arcane secret or two. Nevertheless, when I see the show, which I have done about ninety-seven times, I still gaze in amazement with the awe-struck wonder of an adult child, which, unfortunately, is what all three of us are.

Let us start at the beginning. Penn never drinks or smokes but he has been known to eat fire. Teller doesn't talk; he swears. And, it should be noted, he has the balls of a blind lion tamer.

Teller is such a genius he didn't even know he was a Jew until quite recently. I knew he was Jewish the first time I saw him. He reminded me spiritually of Houdini, who, as you may know, was a Hungarian Jew named Ehrich Weiss. Penn, of course, is not Jewish and he likes to keep it that way.

They are both certified geniuses, and that's one reason they're my friends, as well as having been anointed visiting scholars at MIT, which is the highest honor that institution bestows. They have recently been named two of the funniest people alive by *Entertainment Weekly* magazine. I don't know if I'd go that far, but they are funny enough to make you shit standing.

Penn is about nine feet tall and I first met him when he came to a book signing of mine at the Las Vegas Library (yes, they have one.) He told me, "I'm forty-four but I read at the forty-six-year-old level." I borrowed the line—I mean, stole it—and proceeded to use it relentlessly. It didn't take long in our blossoming relationship for Penn to make it abundantly clear to me that he was an atheist. I told him, "That's fine, but when you die, your tombstone will have to read: 'All dressed up and no place to go.' Penn did not find this particularly humorous. He is a serious atheist. Teller, I've since learned, is also an atheist. I don't make any moral judgments on either of them; I just believe I'm blessed and the Lord is working through me to reach others.

Teller's name is just that. Teller. Even his passport says only one word, "Teller." I have personally confirmed this on a recent trip we took to Lower Baboon's Asshole. But aside from personal quirks and spiritual trivia, it is ironic to say the least that Penn and Teller live in Vegas but do not gamble. Well, that's not quite correct. They gamble every night when they do their show at the Rio.

Some of the things they do in the show are merely entertaining, some seem baffling, and some appear to be truly death-defying. But what makes Penn and Teller remarkable is that they deliberately perform and stage a very nonglitzy, non-Vegas act in Vegas, yet it's sold out virtually every night. In a sense it is truth in magic. The tone is not dissimilar to their Showtime series *Penn & Teller: Bullshit!* That show is confrontational and controversial and tackles the frauds and fakes behind such topics as alien abduction, feng shui, and talking to the dead. It has received eleven Emmy nominations, including two in 2007, and the 2004 WGA Award for Outstanding Comedy/Variety Series. In mainstream, bottom-line Las Vegas, however, the temptation would be to edit, censor, or tone down the act. But Penn and Teller refuse to be tempted, and their instincts and integrity have turned their Vegas show into a financial pleasure.

Take it from the Kinkstah. If you're in Vegas, you really need to see this show at least once in your life. It will amaze you.

As far as animals go, Penn and Teller have made perfect pet choices for magicians. Penn has turtles (whose heads are always going into their shells—now you see it, now you don't), and Teller has blue spiny lizards, who change colors at seminal moments.

Penn and his wife, Emily, have two children and two turtles. Their daughter's name is Moxie Crimefighter Jillette. His son's name is Zolten. "Zolten is a common Hungarian name," says Penn. "It's my wife's maiden name. And, most important, it's the name of Dracula's dog.

"The large turtle is Shirley Temple," he says. "The smaller one, I'm waiting for the children to name." I've met Penn's

"I hate kids."

"Can't you see I'm eating my young?"

kids on several occasions and they're smart, cute little boogers. They do seem, however, perhaps a little slow at naming turtles.

In the photo Teller observes Fensterbenster, a female blue spiny lizard (on cage above), and Fonebone (on wooden ledge below). "Fonebone," says Teller, "turns vivid blue when he's horny, which is almost always.

"These lizards fuck all the time, and have so far produced one litter, of which seven were rescued (the parents like to eat their young) and six have survived and are growing to maturity."

"One pill makes you larger, and one pill makes you small.
And the ones that mother gives you don't do anything at all."

ANN RICHARDS

WHEN ANN RICHARDS was elected governor of Texas in 1990, she was only the second female governor Texas had ever had. The first one, almost sixty years earlier, was Ma Ferguson who, regarding bilingual education, once famously said, "If English was good enough for Jesus Christ, it's good enough for Texas." Ann Richards was known for saying some pretty colorful things herself, but she also brought spirit, wit, and vitality to the governorship that Texas hadn't seen since, well, Ma Ferguson.

Ann grew up in Waco, attended Baylor University on a debate scholarship, and moved to Austin, where she received a teaching certificate from the University of Texas. She taught social studies and history at Fulmore Junior High School in Austin, but politics pulled her away. She campaigned for progressive and liberal local candidates, like Henry B. Gonzalez, Ralph Yarborough, and future U.S. District Judge Sarah T. Hughes. She worked to elect such liberal Democrats to the legislature as Sarah Weddington and Wilhelmina Delco. She also presented training sessions and workshops all over the state to teach campaign techniques to women candidates and campaign workers.

After winning the Democratic primary in 1982 for state treasurer, Ann beat her Republican opponent that year to become the first woman to win statewide office in Texas in more than fifty years. In 1988 she was reelected.

Richards's keynote address at the Democratic National Convention in 1988 really put her on the map nationally. She came down hard on the Reagan administration and Reagan's vice president, George H. W. Bush. Her Texas charm and witty remarks won the day. "Poor George," she said. "He can't help it. He was born with a silver foot in his mouth." She also said something that is just as true today as it was back then: "When we pay billions for planes that won't fly, billions for tanks that won't fire, and billions for systems that won't work, that old dog won't hunt. And you don't have to be from Waco to know that when the Pentagon makes crooks rich and doesn't make America strong, that it's a bum deal." Amen, Sister!

In 1990, Ann Richards was elected governor of Texas. She reformed the state bureaucracy, saving $6 billion. She also reformed the Texas prison system, increasing prison space, reducing the number of violent offenders released, and establishing substance abuse programs for the inmates. Treatment for minor offenders, not incarceration, she felt, was the answer to massive prison overcrowding in Texas. It's still the answer, if anybody's listening.

One of the reasons, I believe, that Ann Richards was so effective governing what has largely become a red state was her basic integrity and her reliance upon people like Barbara Jordan, the first black U.S. congresswoman elected from the South. Barbara Jordan is as close as Texas has ever gotten to having a modern-day statesman. She was, for all practical and spiritual purposes, Ann Richards's mentor. Barbara's grandfather, who ran a junkyard in Houston, once told her some wise words for all political leaders. Barbara was only five years old at the time, but she later passed along this wisdom to Ann: "Love humanity, but don't trust 'em. That," her grandfather contended, "is the true message of Jesus."

Though Ann's strong code of ethics may have been steeled and shaped by people like Barbara Jordan, her laserlike wit was all her own. Ann was that rare bird—a true feminist with a supersized sense of humor. She was known for her big hair, big laugh, and big dreams for Texas. She was not hesitant to mix humor with politics, something terribly lacking in today's cowardly, politically correct crowd.

During the campaign she was asked about the concealed-weapons bill. Someone posed the question to her, "Wouldn't the women of Texas feel better if they could carry guns in their purses?" Ann replied, "Well, I'm not a sexist, but there is not a woman in this state who could find a gun in her handbag, much less lipstick."

One of her most famous and oft-quoted lines was regarding a cause close to her heart, women in politics. In her keynote address to the DNC she observed, "Ginger Rogers did everything Fred Astaire did. She just did it backwards and in high heels."

And then there's this, on November 15, 1998, from the *Fort Worth Star Telegram*: "Kinky saved his first animal in 1979 when he rescued a cat from a shoebox in Chinatown, but he didn't get nonprofit status until spring. That came after he smooth-talked his buddy Willie Nelson and his pal, former Gov. Ann Richards, into helping him form a board of directors for the Utopia Animal Rescue Ranch. Richards told Kinky, 'I hope this isn't something I'm going to regret for the rest of my life.'"

It won't be, Ann. I promise.

P.S. After months of investigative research, I have yet to determine the name of Ann's little bunny (seen in the photo with her parents). Like the unknown soldier, like Ann herself, this cherished childhood friend is honored and acknowledged here.

BILLIE HOLIDAY

and MISTER

*I'm always making a comeback but nobody ever
tells me where I've been.*

—Billie Holiday

I ONCE ASKED WILLIE Nelson who his main influence was
when it came to vocal style. Without hesitation he said,
Frank Sinatra. Frank Sinatra, when asked the same question,
responded, Billie Holiday. When Billie Holiday was asked
who was the main influence on her vocal stylings, she answered, "Louis Armstrong's horn." Just another family tree
that grew in America. And so the fragile torch of flickering
genius is passed or, perhaps more accurately, picked up out
of the dust and borne into the future.

John Hammond, talent scout, writer, and producer,

"discovered" Billie Holiday in 1933 singing for tips at a club in Harlem. He reported that she was the greatest singer he'd ever heard. The story goes that Billie, penniless and facing eviction, sang "Travelin' All Alone" and reduced the audience to tears. It would not be the last time this would happen. Indeed, considered by many to be the greatest jazz vocalist of all time, her life would be fraught with the highs and lows of triumph and tragedy.

Billie Holiday took her name from Billie Dove, an actress she liked, and Clarence Holiday, her probable father. Her mother became pregnant with her at thirteen, both were thrown out of her mother's parents' home, and from there it was the poorest section of Baltimore, reform school, brothels, drugs, a string of abusive men, racism, sexism, and through it all, like a silver thread uplifting the soul, was music.

Strongly inspired by instrumentalists, she pioneered her own way of manipulating wording and tempo to create a more personal, intimate approach to singing. Indeed, Billie Holiday was a seminal influence upon jazz and pop singing. Holiday's amazing method of improvising the melody line to fit the emotion was revolutionary. Though she wrote only a handful of songs herself, some of them have become jazz standards, for instance, "God Bless the Child" and "Lady Sings the Blues."

Through Hammond, Holiday made her recording debut

"No bone, no backstage pass."

in 1933 with Benny Goodman. She went on to work with Teddy Wilson, Duke Ellington, her saxophonist and soul mate Lester Young, Count Basie (1937), and Artie Shaw (1938). Working with Shaw was significant not just musically. In doing so she became among the first black women to perform with a white orchestra. In those days, that was progress.

She began using hard drugs in the early forties and was jailed on drug charges in 1947. She served eight months, and when she got out her NYC Cabaret Card was revoked, preventing her from performing in any place that served alcohol for the last twelve years of her life. On November 10, 1956, when segregation was still a scourge in America, she played a sold out concert at Carnegie Hall. This was a great accomplishment for any artist, especially a black woman at that time.

On May 31, 1959, she was arrested for drug possession as she lay dying at Metropolitan Hospital in New York. She remained under police guard at the hospital until she died of cirrhosis of the liver on July 17. Although she'd earned a substantial income, she had been progressively swindled in the last years of her life, as well as spending the money on drugs and alcohol. She died at age forty-four with seventy cents to her name.

In 1987, Billie Holiday posthumously received the Grammy Lifetime Achievement Award. In 1994, the United

States Postal Service introduced a Billie Holiday postage stamp. In 1999, VH1 picked its hundred greatest women in rock and roll, and Billie ranked number 6. In 2000, she was inducted into the Rock and Roll Hall of Fame.

Billie Holiday felt a great kinship with animals. There is this from *JazzTimes*: "She loves dogs. She always had a pet. One time we were working on 125th Street, at a place called the Apollo Bar, which was near to the Apollo Theater. She came in there one night, I'll never forget it, because she came in with her boxer, Mister, and it was just a beautiful dog. They let her come in with the dog and everything. She came in the back and she sat at a table and she had her dog sitting right next to her. It was great because I'm sure they wouldn't have allowed anyone else to bring a dog in there but they allowed her because she was Billie."

And this, on Mister: "Mister was the best hang-out dog on earth," band member Big Stump informed her biographer, Donald Clarke. "Mister would sit backstage near where he could hear Lady's voice. As long as he heard her voice, he's happy." It was said that Holiday shared everything, including heroin, with Mister.

San Francisco's Fillmore District was a booming black neighborhood during and after World War II. Jimbo's Bop City at 1690 Post Street had an interesting array of performers after hours (from 2:00 A.M. to 6:00 A.M.). The short list included Billie Holiday, Duke Ellington, Miles Davis, Dizzy

Gillespie, Charlie Parker, Count Basie, Dinah Washington, John Coltrane, and Lenny Bruce. Some of the folks who hung out at Jimbo's: Joe Louis, Marilyn Monroe, Sammy Davis Jr., Kim Novak, Clint Eastwood (he used to sneak in as a sixteen-year-old). Jimbo's was where Louis Armstrong went to check out Charlie Parker. This was the only known time the two musicians were under the same roof at the same time.

Fillmore memories: Billie Holiday, coatless and weeping, having just wrapped up her dead dog, Mister, in her floor-length mink coat and cremated them both. "What do a dog do to you, to make you feel so bad?" Jimbo wonders.

TOM WAITS *and* GINGER

TOM WAITS DOES not have a *good* voice; like Bob Dylan and Willie Nelson, he has a *great* voice. Not all music critics necessarily agree, of course. One said Tom's voice "sounds like it was soaked in a vat of bourbon, left hanging in a smokehouse for a few months, and then taken outside and run over with a car." All that notwithstanding, I would just say that as other voices harmonize sweetly into oblivion, Tom's has all the spiritual timbre of a true voice in the wilderness, a voice that remains, in the long-ago loneliness of the horseshit and wild honey that is yesterday, yet a voice forever finding new heads and new hearts.

Waits's audiences are amazing in themselves. They are not the throngs of nostalgia-seeking lawyers; they are not the fallow youth who are there to say they've been there. They are, for the most part, young truth seekers who have found a kindred spirit. Tom can play almost any place in

"You take the high road, I'll take the low road."

the world and they will come—not driven by radio or record company promotional bullshit, but because they are some kind of weird indigo children who've been here before and know something will be delivered, and it always is. Tom Waits is a great teacher of truth that is tragic and music that is magic.

Tom and I had a lot of fun wasting time and ourselves in the Los Angeles of the seventies. That Los Angeles doesn't exist anymore, but Waits and I still do, and I believe it's because we both always remained "in character," dressing, acting, and becoming more who we were all the time, wearing sunglasses twenty-four hours a day BBB (before the Blues Brothers), and never, ever playing golf in the afternoons with record company executives.

Tom in those years famously lived at the Tropicana Hotel on Sunset Boulevard. He had a small, spartan room, the only accoutrement being a stove, which he used only to light his cigarettes. He drank cheap wine, hung out at seedy, soulful bars, and wrote great songs about the people and places most of us never get to know. I admired his bohemian lifestyle back then and, frankly, I still do. His spiritual home always seemed to be at the corner of Fifth and Vermouth.

Tom has won two Grammys, for *Bone Machine* and *Mule Variations*, been nominated for an Academy Award for his sound track on *One from the Heart*, and had songs recorded by many other artists, including Rod Stewart ("Downtown

Train") the Eagles ("Ol' 55"), and Bruce Springsteen ("Jersey Girl)." The influence of his work upon artists, songwriters, musicians, and young people in general has been incalculable.

"Mostly I straddle reality and the imagination," he says. "My reality needs imagination like a bulb needs a socket. My imagination needs reality like a blind man needs a cane."

The reality is that Tom Waits has always walked his own road in a world that has become increasingly sanitized, homogenized, and trivialized. And why is the world like it is? "We are buried beneath the weight of information, which is being confused with knowledge," he says. "Quantity is being confused with abundance, and wealth with happiness. Leona Helmsley's dog made twelve million last year and Dean McLaine, a farmer in Ohio, made thirty thousand. It's just a gigantic version of the madness that grows in every one of our brains. We are monkeys with money and guns."

I agree with Tom about the state of the world, but I believe Leona Helmsley's dog probably earned his $12 million. Tom's dog, Ginger, is no doubt much happier just rambling down a country road listening to Tom playing the one-string violin, an archaic instrument in this modern world, perhaps, but a private concert nonetheless.

I can't remember any animal-related stories regarding Tom from the '70s, but I have difficulty remembering anything from the '70s. Thusly I have consulted our mutual friend, Chuck E. Weiss, who was the inspiration for the song

"Chuck E.'s in Love" and the head honcho of the legendary
L.A. band Chuck E. Weiss and the Goddamn Liars.

Chuck E. informs me that he recalls there always being a
lot of stray cats (of the four-legged variety) hanging around
Tom wherever he lived. This fact alone is a sign of good
character, I believe. Chuck E. also claims that Tom once had
a white rat as a pet, and when he died, "Tom had him stuffed
like his hero Roy Rogers did with Trigger. Every once in a
while he'd put him lovingly on his shoulder.

"I lived at the Tropicana, too," says Chuck E., "in a broom
closet on the floor right below Tom. It was around 1977 at
three o'clock in the morning when I hear loud banging and
scratching noises on my door. I open the door and I see an
image I will never forget. There is a Great Dane bigger than
the Hound of the Baskervilles and he's dragging a drunken
musician friend named Sparky by the collar, and clearly the
dog is very horny and is trying to hump Sparky. Then I realize that Tom is standing there stark naked, brandishing a
broom, frantically trying to beat the dog off of Sparky before
he consummates the act. It is an image I will never forget as
long as I live."

"Oh, no! Not the paparazzi again!"

LILY TOMLIN *and* TESS

L ILY TOMLIN HAS created so many enduring characters and is such a versatile comedic chameleon, it is not surprising that her pets might develop multiple personalities as well. We will explore this phenomenon momentarily with a distinguished dog psychologist, but first let's look at Lily, who has done just about everything you can do and yet, by her own admission, is still getting her act together and taking it on the road.

Lily Tomlin is loved by many for many different reasons. Some are enchanted with one of her earliest breakthrough characters, Ernestine, the wisecracking, gum-chewing, snorting telephone operator who reappears throughout Lily's life and career. What some don't know is that Lily once turned down $500,000 to play Ernestine in an AT&T commercial. Instead, she appeared as Ernestine for nothing in a *Saturday Night Live* parody commercial proclaiming, "We don't care! We don't have to! We're the phone company!"

Some know Lily from her many motion pictures, including *The Incredible Shrinking Woman*, *Nine to Five*, *Nashville* (for which she was nominated for an Academy Award), and *All of Me* (with Steve Martin). Some know her for her television roles on everything from *Desperate Housewives* to *The West Wing* to *Murphy Brown* to *Will and Grace* to being the voice of Tammy on *The Simpsons*.

In 1985, Lily won a Tony for her one-woman Broadway show, *The Search for Signs of Intelligent Life in the Universe*. Few performers are more comfortable than Lily is with a live audience. "One time I was performing for an audience of blind people," she said. "They all had their dogs. And their dogs started howling. It was really funny. I live for those moments, those unplanned moments, when you have to do something spontaneous."

For her universe of so many self-created characters, Lily has won a galaxy of awards: six Emmys and two Tonys, a Drama Desk Award and Outer Critics Circle Award, a CableACE Award, two Peabodys, and others too numerous to mention. The award I think is the coolest, however, was given to Lily in 2003. It was the Mark Twain Prize for American Humor.

There was no small amount of humor in Lily's problems with her dog. "Tess was my beautiful, eleven-pound Norwich terrorist," she says. "Tess died in 1993, during the O. J. Simpson trial. She abhorred injustice. The photo of Tess and me appeared in the *National Enquirer*. Tess instinctively resisted the tabloidization of our lives together.

"I loved her and wished I could say she was my best friend. She was my best critic, though. During the time I was on Broadway doing my partner Jane Wagner's play, *The Search for Signs of Intelligent Life in the Universe*, Tess would stay backstage in my dressing room with my costumer, Maddie Wing. Maddie has reported to me that during the show Tess would look at the speaker, listening to my voice coming from the stage, cocking her head this way and that for the entire first act. One act, though, was usually enough, and then she'd demand that the limo take her to the park until the curtain came down."

Indeed, Lily was having so many problems with Tess that she finally consulted the renowned pet therapist to the stars, Warren Eckstein. "Her dog was like working with Sybil," said Eckstein. "The dog had multiple personalities. But then, Lily practices multiple personalities every single day. If I spend ten or fifteen minutes with someone's dog, I would probably know more about them than they wanted me to know."

Having provided Tess with a checkup from the neck up, and having grieved for her almost as long as Mr. Bojangles, Lily continues making people laugh while pondering the condition of the human condition. Yet somehow she's made the time lately for a big-hearted project. It is a crusade, with Bob Barker, to halt the building of a new $42 million elephant enclosure at the Los Angeles Zoo. "How many elephants have to die at the Los Angeles Zoo," asks Barker, "before they come to terms with the fact that it's impossible to have elephants in a zoo and have them remain happy and healthy?"

Sixteen elephants have died there, about half before they reached the age of twenty. In the wild, elephants easily live to be sixty-five or seventy. Lily is fighting not just to move Billy, the elephant in L.A., but also Jenny, in the Dallas Zoo, to wildlife sanctuaries.

"No habitat in a zoo is big enough for an elephant," says Lily. "They are mammoth, majestic, beautiful, and sensitive, and for generations we have put elephants in zoos. It's not humane and it's not rational or responsible."

I say, God bless Lily Tomlin.

BILL CLINTON, SOCKS, and BUDDY

I N THE FALL of 1994, I was minding my business one day, promoting my latest mystery novel at a book signing in Austin at Barnes & Noble. I had just told the crowd that the reading and the signing were free but there would be a two-latte minimum. A guy came up to me and said, "Hey, Kinky. Sign one for the president." I didn't think the book was really going to Bill Clinton, so I signed one of my standard inscriptions, "Yours in Christ" or "See you in hell," and forgot all about it.

Two weeks later, the postmaster in Medina brought me an express envelope and said in an excited tone, "Kinky, you've got a letter from the White Horse Saloon! You know, that place in Nashville where they do all that line dancing on television!" I looked at the envelope. It did not say "White Horse." It said "White House." Inside the envelope was a letter from President Clinton, and at the bottom he had written,

"I have now read *all* of your books—more please—I *really* need the laughs."

That was the beginning of a three-year pen-pal relationship, during which we discussed many things, from foreign affairs to more metaphysical matters. Regarding Israel, the president wrote, "I appreciate what Tom [my dad] said about my friendship to Israel—I have to do it. Jesus was there too, you know!" And speaking of why there are mostly white pigeons in Hawaii, land of mostly brown-skinned people, and dark-colored pigeons in New York, land of mostly white-skinned people, Bill wrote, "The white pigeons are in Hawaii and the dark pigeons are in New York because God seeks balance in all things. People seek logic and symmetry, which are different."

Our friendship culminated in January 1997, when the president invited my father and me to the White House. The event was a gala dinner for more than two hundred people, several of whom commented rather negatively about my wearing a large black cowboy hat in the White House, but I didn't let it get to me. At first I couldn't find my name at the table setting, but when I did, I was surprised to discover that the card next to mine read "The President." Once I sat down next to the president, people stopped bitching about the cowboy hat. They said, "Who is that charming man sitting next to the president?"

Sherry Lansing, then the president of Paramount Pictures, said that Bill had mentioned to her that my books

"Hey, Bill! I just dumped in the Lincoln Bedroom."

would make wonderful movies. "But who," she asked, "do you see playing Kinky?" "I see Lionel Richie," I said.

Before I left the White House that night, as a token of my gratitude, I gave Bill a Cuban cigar. I told him, "Don't think of it as supporting their economy, Mr. President. Think of it as burning their fields."

In 1991, the Clintons adopted Socks the cat, when she jumped into Chelsea's arms as she was leaving the house of her piano teacher in Little Rock. Socks moved into the governor's mansion and from there to the White House, where Socks became the First Cat of the First Family in Clinton's first term.

Socks was known to share his food and water with a stray cat called Slippers. Socks also went to schools, hospitals, and nursing homes to make goodwill visits. Children who visited the White House website during the Clinton administration were guided by a cartoon version of Socks.

**"You didn't hear this from me,
but Buddy also dumped on Air Force One."**

Socks was very popular indeed. So popular that Republican Representative Dan Burton once publicly questioned the use of White House staff, postage, and stationery to answer all the fan mail addressed to the cat.

All this notwithstanding, everything came to an end in 1997 when the Clintons adopted a male, chocolate-colored Labrador retriever named Buddy. Socks and Buddy did not get along, so the two of them had to be kept in separate quarters in the White House. According to Hillary Clinton, "Socks despised Buddy from first sight, instantly and forever." Bill Clinton said, "I did better with the Palestinians and the Israelis than I've done with Socks and Buddy."

About a year after he was out of office, I got a chance to hang out with Bill in Sydney, Australia, at a nightclub called the Basement. We were there with the actor Will Smith to see the horn player Maynard Ferguson, of whom Bill was a big fan. Bill spoke to us almost as if it were a White House briefing, discussing world affairs, particularly AIDS in Africa. I thought then that the only job harder than being president is being a former president.

Bill Clinton is a good man, a much-loved man, who is not perfect. If he has a weakness, it is that he leads with his heart. Being president, inevitably, took its toll upon him. It comes as no surprise, of course. Like they say, "If you want a friend in Washington, get a dog."

"Without me, he's nothing."

TOM ROBBINS *and*
BLINI TOMATO TITANIUM

TOM ROBBINS AND I first met about twenty years ago when we were stuck in a green room in L.A. with Bishop Desmond Tutu. Bishop Tutu was cordial but didn't have time for the likes of Tom and myself. He also had a large entourage that completely surrounded him.

"He must be very short," Tom said at the time. "You can't even see him."

Tom and I retired into a corner, smoked cigars (which was still possible in L.A. back then), chatted for a while, and I gave Tom my card (which read, "Kinky Friedman is allowed to walk on the grounds unattended," followed by my address).

Many years later I received a letter from Tom, and a sprightly pen-pal relationship sprung up between the two men of letters until life got in the way and it ended, as all good things must. I have yet to hear from Bishop Tutu, but I live in hope.

Like the wayward son of literature, however, Tom Robbins has carried on. This year, Tom published his tenth book. It is a children's book, he tells me. Its title: *B Is for Beer*.

Tom Robbins remains an extremely reclusive man of mystery and he likes to keep it that way. His works are highly cherished by readers for, among other things, the way he manages to mix fantasy, spirituality, sexuality, humor, and poetry in combinations that have never been seen before in literature. I have yet to meet an intelligent woman who does not love Tom Robbins.

"I think too much is known about me already," he says. "I think biographical information can get in the way of the reading experience. Anyway, you'll never learn anything truthful about me on the Net. Somewhere there's a writer who wears a tweed jacket, has an English sheepdog, smokes a pipe, and has a mousy wife in the next room writing a doctorate thesis on Andrew Marvell, but that's not me."

I asked Tom how he's managed not to blow his fucking head off, living at an undisclosed location in the Pacific Northwest where it rains virtually all the time.

"The rain that we have in the Pacific Northwest, it's not a torrential kind of rain, for the most part. It's very soft. It's a wonderful climate for a writer because it reduces temptation. It keeps you indoors. It turns you inward. It makes you introspective. And there's something very cozy and romantic about it, I find. People all around me in the middle of winter are threatening suicide because the rain falls day after day after day, and I just get happier and happier."

I asked the author of *Even Cowgirls Get the Blues* if it's true that he understands women better than any other man on earth, including Hugh Hefner.

"There are people who think I understand women. Actually, I understand about twenty-three out of about four billion. I don't claim to understand them in general. I do tend to prefer their company.

"At the time when my first two books were published, I did not grant interviews or make public appearances and my photograph was not widely disseminated, so because I wrote from a female perspective, a lot of people did think that I was actually a woman. I took this as a compliment.

"My method of writing is—well, I don't recommend it to anyone. It works for me but I think it's probably a really crazy way to write. I write everything in longhand. I like to watch the ink soak into the wood pulp. When you write as slowly as I do, you don't go back and change scenes. I'll go back and change individual words, maybe even a phrase here and there. There's not a word in any of my books that I haven't gone over thirty or forty times. Each individual word. One reason I don't go back and read them later, even after all that, is that I keep coming across words that I would like to change.

"I don't plot in advance. When I begin a book I have only the vaguest sense of how the plot is going to shape itself and no sense at all of how it's going to end. You wouldn't know it from reading the book, because the end ties in with the beginning, I think, absolutely seamlessly and smoothly. But when I introduced those themes at the beginning of the book, I had no idea where it was going to take me. That's the adventure of it for me. That's the fun of it. But to make it appear as if I knew everything in the beginning demands a tremendous amount of concentration and energy. At the end of every writing day I feel like I've been wrestling in radioactive quicksand with Xena the Warrior Princess and her five fat uncles."

I asked Tom about his pet, the toy Yorkshire terrier named Blini Tomato Titanium.

"She weighs four pounds," he said, "with a personality the size of King Kong."

"How did she get her name?" I wondered. "I mean, I'm not trying to pry."

"I knew that was her name when I first saw her."

"How old is Blini Tomato Titanium?"

"She'll be four on January 29th," said Tom without hesitation.

"How did you get her?"

"I'm not supportin their economy, I'm burnin their fields."

"My wife, Alexa, is a psychic. She saw her spirit when she was just two inches long when they were going to let her die at a puppy mill in Iowa. A worker there took her home, kept her in a laundry room, fed her with an eyedropper, and Alexa bought her over the Internet.

"I told her I didn't want a dog, I'd never had a dog, and if she got this one, it would have to stay in her office. I just never saw the point of having pets. I used to mock people who were hung up on their pets. Now I'm worse than they ever were. I can't even go to the post office without taking her with me. She's opened up my heart. I've seen the light."

Tom claims he's cried only twice in his adult life, at the end of the movie *Born on the Fourth of July* and when Blini Tomato Titanium was sick and they thought they were going to lose her.

Talking on the phone with Tom was a very pleasant experience. I could imagine him there at some undisclosed location in the Pacific Northwest, luxuriating in the rain in his tweed jacket with his English sheepdog, smoking his pipe—no, that's not him.

"You know," I said, "my father's name was Tom. I wonder if you'd consider being a father figure for me?"

"I wish my father's name had been Kinky," he said. "I might've had a more interesting childhood."

LEVON HELM and MUDDY

IN 1954, WHEN Levon Helm was fourteen years old, he went to nearby Helena, Arkansas, to see a show starring Johnny Cash and Carl Perkins. Also on the bill was a young guy named Elvis Presley who played rockabilly with Scotty Moore on guitar and Bill Black on stand-up bass. Elvis did not have a drummer at the time.

One year later, Levon saw Elvis again. Though he hadn't hit the big time yet, Elvis had D. J. Fontana with him on drums and Bill Black on electric bass. Levon saw the people jumping out of their seats and dancing in the aisles, and he was amazed at the difference made by the change in the instrumentation. He was a fifteen-year-old kid but he'd regularly won 4-H Club talent contests with guitar and harmonica and his sister Linda on bass, and he knew he was watching history in the making.

He formed his own rock band, the Jungle Bush Beaters, when he was a junior in high school, and at seventeen, after watching Jerry Lee Lewis's drummer, Jimmy Van Eaton, he decided to become a drummer, and damned if he didn't become one of the very greatest in the world. He was loaded with natural-born musical talent, but he did have other skills. He was also the tractor-driving champion of Arkansas.

Conway Twitty gave Levon some help, and then Ronnie Hawkins hired him as drummer for the Hawks in 1957. By the early sixties, they'd picked up four Canadian musicians, Rick Danko, Richard Manuel, Garth Hudson, and Robbie Robertson. After a time, they separated from Ronnie Hawkins and, in 1965, Bob Dylan hired the band to help him go electric.

"The drummer's stool is the best seat in the house," Levon once said, "because you can see the musicians and the audience simultaneously." Interestingly, Ringo Starr, on the same subject, said, "My only regret is that I never got to see the Beatles." Is the glass half full or half empty, or are we all half full of shit?

All this notwithstanding, Bob, Levon, and the band got booed every night in a baptism of fire delivered by the musically myopic, die-hard Dylan folk fans. After that the band retired to Woodstock, rented a large pink house, and in July

"Do you always walk like that?"

of 1968 released their first album, *Music from Big Pink*, which knocked just about everybody's dick to his watch pocket. Because the Woodstockians called them the band, they called themselves the Band. The second album—titled, of all things, *The Band*—was possibly even better. The music was unique, the harmonies were incomparable, and the songs were Southern born, Southern bred, and Southern fried—and pure Levon.

The Band went on to make seven albums, and Elton John was so impressed he recorded a tribute song in 1971 called simply "Levon." Muddy Waters was impressed enough to come to Levon's new studio in Woodstock, the Barn, and record an album with him. *Muddy Waters in Woodstock* was released in 1975 and promptly won a Grammy.

On Thanksgiving of 1976, way too soon, the Band gave its farewell concert called "The Last Waltz." I was privileged to be backstage. I was also privileged to be so high I needed a stepladder to scratch my ass. It was a beautiful, bittersweet night with a galaxy of stars, and it was the last time I would see my favorites, Levon, Rick Danko, and Richard Manuel, perform together.

Levon made his first film appearance in 1980, as Loretta Lynn's father in *Coal Miner's Daughter*. Latte-sipping critics everywhere loved his "authenticity." Levon has gone on to appear in numerous other movies, including *The Right Stuff*,

Shooter, and *The Three Burials of Melquiades Estrada* with Tommy Lee Jones.

In *The Electric Mist*, Levon's latest movie, he portrays the Confederate general John Bell Hood. While lensing in Louisiana, Levon met Lucy, "a Catahoula hound who may be the camp dog in the movie or may make the cutting-room floor." Either way, Levon took Lucy back to Woodstock to meet his dog Muddy.

"We named Muddy in honor of Muddy Waters," says Levon, "and he lives up to his name. We also call him 'Mud the Stud' because he's now had two litters with Lucy, eight puppies and nine puppies, and all to good homes.

"Muddy knows Woodstock better than I do. He picks up his friend Jake, the dog from down the street, and they go down to town to the bank. The bank gives drive-thru customers dog bones if they see that you've got a dog. So Muddy and Jake just go down there and rear up on the call box, bangin' for a bone.

"Muddy also used to visit the neighbor's dog, who was sick with cancer. Muddy'd walk by their house, scratch on the door, and when they let him in, he'd lie next to the sick dog for several hours, then get up and go home. The dog finally died and now Muddy just looks at the house as we walk by but he doesn't try to go in anymore."

When I played Levon's famous "Midnight Ramble" at the

Barn in Woodstock recently, I not only got the chance to hang out with my old friend Levon, but I also got to meet Muddy in person. I can tell you, he's all Levon says he is. Not only that, but Muddy has an all-access pass. He goes absolutely anywhere he wants and, not surprisingly, one of the places he likes to be the most is onstage.

JOHNNY CASH *and* SNORKLE

I WAS NOT YET in my teens when Johnny Cash became my hero. The year might've been 1956 or 1957, and I'd just learned how to play the guitar as well as I would ever learn to play it. Johnny Cash did not play it much better, of course, but he had the Tennessee Two, Luther Perkins and Marshall Grant.

Nor did Johnny have what we would call a trained voice or possibly even a good voice. But he had life and sadness and courage and gravel in his voice, and besides, there was something else distinctive about his voice. It spoke to twelve-year-old guitar pickers.

Johnny Cash's chords and chord progressions were simple but very catchy. Several veteran record producers in Nashville have told me that there was an almost unconscious reason why his style was so infectious and basic, perhaps best exemplified by the song "I Walk the Line." They say

Cash's signature musical style evolved from his assignment in the early fifties to a U.S. Air Force Security Service unit at Landsberg, Germany, where he was intensely immersed as a Morse code decoder of transmissions from the Russian military. Once I'd heard this, I listened again to "I Walk the Line" and other Cash songs and heard the hypnotic Morse code influence as one of the things that set him apart from many other country stars. Another thing that set him apart, of course, was his unparalleled, unbridled, at times uncontrollable raw talent.

Like many artists who live on the road in an endless chain of one-night stands, Johnny Cash often took more pills than Alice in Wonderland. The story goes that Cash had just recorded "I Walk the Line," then promptly left Nashville to do a string of dates in Florida. He happened to hear the song on the radio and became highly agitato. He called his manager in Nashville and let him have it. The song wasn't ready, it wasn't finished, it never should've been released, Cash insisted. "I don't want it played on the radio like it is," Cash reportedly told his manager. "Pull all the copies back in," he demanded. "That would be a little difficult," his manager said. "It's already #1 in over two hundred markets."

One measure of Johnny Cash's sustained success is that he's loved, respected, and admired by different generations for different reasons. He's won seventeen Grammys and has been inducted into Nashville Songwriters Hall of Fame

(1977), the Country Music Hall of Fame (1980), and the Rock and Roll Hall of Fame (1992). Only three other artists share the honor of being in all three halls of fame: Hank Williams Sr., Jimmie Rodgers, and Bill Monroe. Of these, only Cash was inducted into the Rock and Roll Hall of Fame in the regular manner. The others were inducted as "early influences."

In my life, however, Johnny Cash was definitely one of my early influences. I've noticed that young people today seem to be largely unfamiliar with what I consider to be his greatest work; they genuinely love Johnny Cash, but for different songs and different reasons. This, of itself, is a great compliment to the man. His spiritual wingspan is considerable and he has transcended the forms and limitations of art itself and moved into the hearts of the people.

Music is a very subjective thing, but many Johnny Cash songs remain in my consciousness or maybe my soul like lingering chords of childhood. When I think of the Man in Black, I think of the brilliant delivery of the funny, insightful, Shel Silverstein–penned musical epic, "A Boy Named Sue." Not many artists could bring that one home, or would have recognized it for its cultural importance. And "Folsum Prison Blues," a perfect, simple song about the real meaning of freedom. Yet "I Still Miss Someone" is Cash's favorite of all his works, and I deeply suspect it to have been a true personal statement for all of his life. It's one of those little feelings that lie behind and help create what the world considers to be true greatness.

My favorites, I suspect, remain mostly unknown to many Johnny Cash fans today. That's because they're pretty green and I'm pretty old. And yet we all feel the same way about Johnny Cash. He has struggled with his demons and, as a result, his life is inspirational, and his legacy is all the greater for it.

"Come In, Stranger" was one of the first songs I ever learned to play on the guitar. Timeless, beautiful song. "Cry, Cry, Cry," "Big River," "Five Feet High and Risin'," "Don't Take Your Guns to Town," and "Don't Step on Mama's Roses" are just a few of the classics and part of the essence of the artist. My father's all-time favorite was "Pickin' Time," a story about what it was like to try to make a living picking cotton (which Cash did when he was just five years old). The song describes how very tough life is but holds the promise of better things ahead come pickin' time. The song's last verse is as follows:

Last Sunday mornin' when they passed the hat
It was still nearly empty back where I sat
But the preacher smiled and said that's fine
The Lord'll wait til Pickin' Time.

Pictured here is Johnny Cash, his pet pig, Snorkle, and an unidentified turkey.

"Who invited this turkey for lunch?"

Von Kinky Family Singers. Painting by Dusty Pendleton

PHOTO CREDITS

Page 106: Photo by Harry Benson

Page 110: Photo courtesy of Larry Dierker

Page 114: Photo courtesy of The Mark Twain House & Museum, Hartford, Conn.

Page 120: © Mark Perlstein/Time & Life Pictures/Getty Images

Page 131: Photo by Kent Perkins

Page 134: Photo by Karla Thomas

Page 138: Photo by Michael Childress

Pages 142 and 146: Photos courtesy of Mac and Cat Rebennack

Page 148: Photo by Syndey Byrd

Page 153: Photo by Bill Thorup

Pages 156 and 160: Photos courtesy of Penn Jillette

Page 161: Photo courtesy of Teller

Page 162: Photo courtesy of Ellen Richards

Page 169: Photo by William P. Gottlieb

Page 174: Photograph by Michael O'Brien

Page 178: Photo courtesy of Lily Tomlin

Page 185: © Barbara Kinney/Time & Life Pictures/Getty Images

Page 186: © Tim Sloan/AFP/Getty Images

Pages 188 and 193: Photos by Alexa Robbins

Page 197: Photo by Paul La Raia

Page 205: Photo courtesy of Marty Stuart

Page 206: Painting courtesy of Utopia Rescue Ranch